The Lorimer Pocketguide to

London
Birds

120 Species in Full Colour

Written & illustrated by
Jeffrey C. Domm

James Lorimer & Company Ltd., Publishers
Toronto, Ontario
2002

Dedicated to my brother Mark and his family, Michele, Lyndsey and Courtney.

James Lorimer & Company Ltd. acknowledges the support of the Ontario Arts Council. We acknowledge the financial support of the Government of Canada through the Book Publishing Industry Development Program (BPIDP) for our publishing activities.

National Library of Canada Cataloguing in Publication

Domm, Jeffrey C., 1958-
        The Lorimer pocketguide to London birds : 120 species in full colour /
written & illustrated by Jeffrey C. Domm.

Includes index.
ISBN 1-55028-776-1

        1. Birds—Ontario—London—Identification. 2. Bird watching—Ontario—London—Guidebooks. I. Title.

QL685.5.O6D655 2002   598'.09713'26   C2002-903779-4

Cartography: Peggy McCalla

James Lorimer & Company, Publishers
35 Britain Street
Toronto, Ontario M5A 1R7
www.lorimer.ca

Printed and bound in Canada

Introduction

This book is designed to help you identify birds quickly and easily. Each species is given one full page, which includes a colour illustration as well as keys to correct identification of birds seen in the London area. The illustrations are drawn from several sources, including photographs, observations and scientific data. They emphasize the distinguishing features — shape, colour and markings — and each one represents a typical specimen. One should expect to see variation in the colour of a bird's plumage — variation that results from changing seasons and light conditions.

To identify a bird, use the 2-step Bird Finder on pages 4-5, which organizes the species by size and by colour. To become familiar with the graphic symbols used in this book see the "How to use this guide" section on pages 6-7.

Of the more than 400 species recorded in southern Ontario, we have selected 120 familiar birds for this book. They are organized in the taxonomic sequence presented by the American Ornithologists' Union. The wetland and water birds precede the woodland and field birds. Make your own record of bird sightings on the checklist (pages 138-145).

Before setting out on a bird watching excursion, check the weather forecasts. If a storm moves in very quickly, strong winds, rain and cool temperatures can affect the number of birds that you see and can dampen spirits on your expedition. Always take along waterproof clothing as well as your binoculars. For this book, a local birding expert has provided information on Hot Spot Birding Locations that are favoured by local enthusiasts.

Birds of all sizes play an important role in the balance of nature, but their survival is increasingly threatened by unnatural incursions. Preserving habitat diversity is becoming vital as human encroachment extends farther into wildlands. Wetlands have declined because of drainage, farming and urbanization, while forests have been harvested and replaced with housing, roads and industrial development. In addition, habitat has been affected by exotic diseases, alien insects and invasive plants. One of the greatest threats to songbirds is the domestic cat.

This book is intended to expand awareness about birds and their place in nature. You can find out more about local birds and their habitat by contacting one of the many organizations dedicated to their preservation and protection. The best-known birding association in London is McIlwraith Field Naturalists of London. Visit their website at mcilwraith.tripod.ca.

2-Step Bird Finder: Size and Colour

Step 1. Determine the approximate size of bird in relation to page size.
Step 2. Compare overall colour and specific markings and turn to page number.

125 134

43 96

66 65

58 130

40 98

60 73

48 49

74 51

129 99

77 68

53 46

35 41

33 27

37 44

50 25

30 78

69 131

59 56

57 64

34 32

23 24

54 38

21 22

61 29

31 45

20 55

42 26

47 18

36 39

28 19

How to use this guide

Birds don't stay in one place for very long, so it is important to learn a few simple rules to help you identify them quickly. Most often what you see is a bird that is feeding; perhaps it is hopping along the ground or flitting from branch to branch. Maybe it is perched in a tree, preparing to fly away at any second. The visual keys given in this guide focus on the most identifiable features of each bird — colour, outline and size. In addition, there are other behavioural traits that help identify birds at a distance. For inland birds, nesting location is an important indicator of habitat. For shore and water birds, the way the bird feeds and the style of flying are helpful hints.

When you are looking at a bird, first estimate the size, then take note of the shape of the wings, tail, head, beak and feet. Note any particular marks — patches, streaks, stripes and speckles. Watch its movements to see how it flies, hops and feeds.

Legend for visual keys

1 **Size identification** — the rectangle represents the page of this book, and the silhouette of the bird represents its size against this page.

2 **Beak** — the shape of the beak and head can be very helpful in identifying a bird.

3 **Flight characteristics** —

Quick wingbeats

Slow steady wingbeats

Soaring

Wingbeats followed by gliding

4 **Feeding technique** —

Stabs and prodding motion

Grazing and dabbling

Diving and clutching with feet

Diving head first

Dives from water's surface

Tip up feeding

Skims water surface

Feeding

5 **Backyard feeder** — there are two types of bird feeders to which small birds might be attracted.

Backyard Feeder

6 **Birdhouse nester** — some species are happy to make their nest in a manmade house that you hang in your garden.

Birdhouse Nester

7 **Nesting location** (for inland birds only) —

▼ Hollow in ground

▼ Waterside plants

▽ Bushes and thickets

▼ Cavities of trees

▼ Deciduous trees

▼ Conifers and tall trees

▼ Tall, dead, decaying trees

▼ Banks along rivers and ponds

▽ Cliffs and/or rocky ledges

Nesting Location

8 **Egg** — actual size and shape unless otherwise indicated.

9 **Observation calendar** — the bar provides the initial for each of the 12 months of the year. The deeper colour indicates the best months for seeing the species, according to known migration patterns.

Observation Calendar

J F M A M J J A S O N D

Egg: 75%

7

London Birding Hot Spots selected by Pete Read

1 Fanshawe Park Conservation Area

This is a recreation-class park, with camping and many other facilities. In migration periods, a lot of waterfowl use the large artificial lake above the dam. Smaller birds, such as warblers, can be found along the Riverside Trail, which heads downstream from the small parking area on the north side of the river, below the dam. The evergreen plantations within the park sometimes hold wintering finches and crossbills. The park entrance is located off Clarke Road, between Huron Street and Fanshawe Road. Expect user fees in season.

❷ Thames Valley Trail

A long trail follows the Thames River, often along both sides. The trail is particularly well used on the north branch, from the east at Fanshawe Park to the west in Komoka Provincial Park. Many resident riverside birds, such as Catbird, House Wren, Baltimore Oriole and others, nest along the trails. Visit the trails in spring and fall migration as well, since the river acts as a migration corridor for birds. The trails can be accessed from many spots, especially where there are bridges. On the north branch, one north-side access is located at the end of Windermere Road, off Adelaide Street between Kipp's Lane and Fanshawe Road. Turn east at the intersection and park at the dead end. Another access is from Highbury Avenue. Turn onto Killarney Road just north of the bridge and go to the end, where you will turn left at McLean Drive. The first crescent on the south side is Wakefield. Park at the walkway and go down the stairway to the river valley. There is a southside access off Kilally Road. Take Kilally Road west from Highbury Avenue and park about a half kilometre down beside an evergreen woodlot. There is a trail from Edgevalley Road to the river.

❸ Weldon Park

This little park has good trails that cut through mixed habitat. These trails can be rewarding, especially during migration, but also during winter when some birds use the park for food and shelter. Red-bellied Woodpecker and Eastern Wood-Peewee are found in the upland woods. It is located in the community of Arva, north of London along Richmond Street North (Highway 4).

❹ Medway Valley

This is an Environmentally Significant Area, located along the Medway River and running between Fanshawe Park Road and Western Road. Various habitats are seen along its trails. Look for resident birds like Downy Woodpecker and Belted Kingfisher, but also watch for migrants, especially warbler species in mid-May. Best access is on a trail from the west side of the parking lot of the London Museum of Archaeology on Attawandaron Road, reached from Attawandaron Gate, which runs off of Wonderland Road just south of Fanshawe Park Road.

5 Gibbons Park/UWO campus

Popular trails follow the river through this park and up to the University of Western Ontario. Resident birds include Baltimore Oriole, Mallard, swallows and sometimes Great Blue Heron. There is a parking area at the bottom of the hill at the west end of Grosvenor Street, which is reached after travelling a few blocks west of the intersection with Richmond Street, north of Oxford Street.

6 Harris Park

This little park is a groomed, well-used spot, located where the north and south branches of the Thames River meet. At all times of the year, look for waterfowl in the river, just off the parking area below the art gallery. Riverside Drive becomes Dundas Street as you head east, and you can access the park by turning left immediately after crossing the bridge.

7 South Branch Bikeway

This long path goes through many different habitats as it follows the south branch of the Thames River for about eight kilometres, alternating on the north and south banks. Look for migrant species in spring and residents such as Red Cardinal, Gray Catbird and Red-winged Blackbird. Two spots that are good for birds are the first section from the Pottersburg Treatment Plant, where parking is off Hamilton Road, just east of Gore Road, to the Highbury bridge and between the Egerton Street bridge and Adelaide bridge, on either side of the river.

8 Kiwanis Park

The park runs along a creek that empties into the Thames. Paths wander through the various habitats. Look for phoebes, Northern Cardinal and Kingfisher, as well as migrants in spring and fall. Park in the small parking area beside the Gore Road bridge over the creek. Then walk north along the trail on the west side of the Pottersburg Creek. Watch out for trains as you scramble up the embankment and drop down to the other side of the creek. Continue down the other side following paths back to Gore Road.

9 Meadowlily Woods

This Environmentally Significant Area is about 46 hectares of public land with trails leading down to old growth Maple/Beech woodlands along the South Branch of the Thames. It is known for migrating birds (especially warblers) in mid-May, but you can see resident woodland species like Scarlet Tanager, Rose-breasted Grosbeak and Red-bellied Woodpecker. It is located on Meadowlily Road, off Commissioner's Road East, just west of the intersection with Highbury. Park near the gates called "Park Farms," and walk left on the path. There is privately owned land there also, so watch for and obey any signs.

10 Westminster Ponds/Pond Mills Conservation Area

This is a very large and habitat-rich area stretching from Pond Mills Conservation Area through a creek valley to Westminster Ponds Conservation Area. The first has two kettle lakes (Ice Age deep small lakes) on the east end, while the second has three kettle lakes. Resident Great Horned Owl, Song Sparrow, Black-capped Chickadee, Northern Cardinal and many others are found here. It is one of the best places in the London area to see migrant species, from waterfowl in the lakes to warblers in the woods. Pond Mills Conservation Area can be accessed from near the intersection of Southdale Road and Pond Mills Road. Westminster Ponds is located off Wellington Road South, where you can park at the back of the London Tourist Info Centre, north of the intersection with Southdale Road. It is best to cover these places separately, parking at either end and enjoying the sets of ponds.

⑪ Kirk-Cousins Management Area

This is a productive birding area with varied habitat to look through. From the parking lot, walk the trails or scan the area from the viewing stands overlooking the ponds to see waterfowl and herons. Migrants such as warblers, and nesting species like Wood Thrush and robins use the woods. Kirk-Cousins is on Scotland Drive, just east of the intersection with Wellington Road South.

⑫ Greenway Park

This is a large park where hiking trails give access upstream and down on the river. Especially in the winter, look for waterfowl and gull species in the warm spillwater from the Greenway Pollution Plant. Or walk over to the small oxbow pond close to Springbank that may have Gray Catbird in the trees, or Blue Heron in its shallow waters. Parking is accessed off Springbank Drive onto Greenside Avenue. Not in the park but on the other side of the river, a trail follows the river from Cavendish Crescent westward to Wonderland Road. Cavendish is reached from Riverside Drive, just west of the intersection at Wharncliffe Road.

⑬ Springbank Park

An old park with large trees, Springbank has many walking trails that follow the river. It harbours many species of birds, particularly in migration periods. Waterfowl can be found on the river, and woodland species live along the banks. Park off Springbank Drive and walk in from the east entrance, or go farther west and make a turn west onto Commissioner's Road West, to the entrance off that street.

⑭ Warbler Woods

This Environmentally Significant Area consists of hilly woodlands of mainly old growth forest, and contains typical woodland species, such as Wood Thrush, Rose-breasted Grosbeak, American Robin and others. In May, watch for many migrants, especially warblers. The parking area is found on the left just as you ascend the hill heading west on Commissioner's Road West, out of Byron, a community at the west edge of London.

15 Sifton Bog

A remnant of the Ice Age, this acidic bog is rare habitat in southern Ontario. Besides special flora (including leatherleaf and pitcher plant) around the little sphagnum-covered lake, look for resident species, which include American Robin, Black-capped Chickadee and Common Yellowthroat. Parking is in a small lot off the south side of Oxford Street West, just west of the intersection with Hyde Park Road.

6 Komoka Provincial Park

Located along the Thames River at the west edge of London, this large park is mostly a nature preserve with many trails through varied habitat. The bird list comprises about 80 nesting species, including Blue-winged Warbler, Brown Thrasher, Eastern Towhee, and, in the woods, Scarlet Tanager, Blue Jay and others. Savannah and Field sparrows and other field nesters live in the old gravel pit on the north side. Riverside species such as Song Sparrow and Cardinal can also be found. This park is also especially good for spring and fall migrants. To access the south side, there are two main parking areas. The first is off Glendon Drive, just before the bridge in the village of Kilworth, while the second is also off Glendon, just at the intersection of Brigham Road. Commissioner's Road West becomes Glendon (County Road 14) after it leaves London. Gideon Road (Middlesex County Road 3) branches off to the south, heading towards Delaware, not far past a crossroad called Westdel Bourne. For north-side access, continue along Gideon to Komoka Road (Middlesex County Road 16), turn north and go over the bridge. You can park just up at the top of the hill next to the sewage treatment plant. The charging of user fees in season is under review.

17 Komoka Ponds

These old gravel-pit ponds have become resting areas for about 25 species of waterfowl in the spring and fall. Common migrants include American Coot, Ring-necked Duck, wigeon, mergansers, and cormorants. They are located at the northeast corner of the intersection of Komoka Road, Middlesex County Road 16, and Glendon Drive at the lights in Komoka. Glendon is Middlesex County Road 14, an extension of Commissioner's Road West, coming out of London (Byron). Park along either road facing the lake. It is best to bring a viewing scope as the birds can be far away.

18 Delaware Sportsman Pond

This is a great marsh wetland for herons, Wood Duck and Red-winged Blackbird, as well as for species in the surrounding woodlands. Listen for Sora and other rails, and perhaps bitterns. Although access is by permission only, there is a good viewing area overlooking the marsh, from Bringham Road, between Gideon Drive and Longwoods Road. Also known as Middlesex County Road 3, Gideon runs southwest off Commissioner's Road West, heading towards Delaware. Bringham runs south from it, at the corner where the Versa Care nursing home is located.

19 Aylmer Wildlife Management Area

This is a great area for spotting waterfowl, specifically the Tundra Swans that arrive (sometimes by the thousands) in March and early April. The viewing stands offer good views of these tundra nesters. Travel south from Highway 401 (interchange 203) on Elgin Road (County Road 73) to Glencolin Line (County Road 32) and turn east. Then, go over one road and turn left again. This is still County Road 32, though the name has changed to Hacienda Road. Less than one kilometre down this road is the entrance.

20 Springwater Conservation Area

This conservation area is known as a great local birding hot spot that harbours some interesting species. Breeders in the beautiful Carolinian forest include Red-eyed Vireo, Scarlet Tanager, Wood Thrush, and Eastern Wood-Peewee. Drive east of St. Thomas, or west from Aylmer on Highway 3, turning south on Elgin County Road 35, at Orwell. The main entrance is about three kilometres south on the east side of the road.

1 Port Stanley

This is a pretty harbour along Lake Erie and a good spot for migrating waterfowl and gulls. Look out over the lake for ducks and look for rarer gulls, such as Great Black-backed, in the winter. Port Stanley is on Elgin County Road 4, a continuation of Highway 4 in London. It is called Wharncliffe Road and then Colonel Talbot Road as you exit west from London, through the community of Lambeth. As the highway passes south of Highway 401, it becomes county road Sunset Drive. Alternatively, travel on Wellington Road South, which joins Sunset Drive at the south end of St. Thomas. Continue on Sunset Drive through the west part of St. Thomas. Explore the harbour from lakeside accesses on either side of the lift bridge.

2 Hawk Cliff

This is a cliff located along the north shore of Lake Erie. It is a hotspot for hawk migration in the fall. Peak numbers of birds are expected in the second week of September, when thousands pass by just above the land or high in the sky in "kettles" of raptors. If you go on one of the locally advertised viewing weekends when banding of the hawks is organized, banders release captives in front of you, as well as answer your questions. A parking area is located at the south end of Elgin County Road 22, which is also called Fairview Road. Head out of London on Wellington Road South or Colonel Talbot Road, at the west end of the city. Follow the road south as it becomes Sunset Drive (County Road 4). Continue along Sunset as it goes through the southern part of St. Thomas. At the village of Union, take Sparta Line (Elgin County 27) east one road, then turn south onto Fairview (Elgin County Road 22). Continue to the lake.

23 Longwoods Conservation Area

A variety of habitats are found in Longwoods, from open fields to wet woods, from ravine to marsh. It is located west of London on Longwoods Road (Middlesex County Road 2). Here you can find migrants in season, or Gray Catbird, Northern Cardinal, and Black-capped Chickadee all year. You can also spot marsh birds, such as Swamp Sparrow and Red-winged Blackbird. From the community of Lambeth go west on Longwoods Road. Watch for the entrance on the north side of the road about five kilometres past the village of Delaware. Expect user fees in season.

24 Middlesex County Forests/Skunk's Misery

West of London, near the town of Newbury, there are many hectares of county-owned wet woodland, as well as oak forests. Many special species of birds can be found there, including Chestnut-sided Warbler and Least Flycatcher. Other nesters include Red-eyed Vireo, Redstart and Ovenbird. A user-management plan is in the works and there are many proposed access trails off several roads in the area, bounded by Concession Road in the north, Trillium Road in the south, Hagerty Road in the east and Sassafras Road in the west. Keep off posted lands and take along boots for the wet trails and insect repellent in bug season.

25 The Pinery Provincial Park

This is an excellent park for access to Lake Huron. It is a great place to bird, either on the trails through the oak-savannah habitat, or by looking out on the lake. It is good for nesting species such as Black-capped Chickadee, Rose-breasted Grosbeak and many others, but also for migrants and winter birds. From London, travel west to Middlesex Road 81, either on Middlesex Road 22 (Fanshawe Park Road in London, then Egremont Drive when it becomes Road 22), or along Highway 402. Go north on 81, following it through Parkhill, and turn west onto the Greenway Drive, about 10 kilometres north of town. Drive to Highway 21. Just a quick turn to the west finds you at the gates of this popular park. Expect user fees in season.

Contents

Common Loon
Gavia immer

Size Identification

Beak

Flying

Feeding

Observation Calendar
J F M A M J J A S O N D

Male/Female: *Summer*: Black head and neck with white banded neck ring; thick grey sharp bill; red eyes; white chest and belly; black back and white spotted wings; black feet and legs. *Winter*: Contrasting blacks and whites muted to dark dull brown. In flight: large feet trail behind tail feathers; quick wing beats close to water's surface; takes off from water by running across surface.

Did you know? Loons can remain underwater for more than 5 minutes. They dive to feed and to avoid danger.

Voice: Drawn out *lou-lou-lou-lou*-like yodelling, often at dusk or dawn.
Food: Small fish.
Nest/Eggs: Mound built with aquatic plants, mostly on islands. 2 eggs.

Egg: 75%

18

Double-crested Cormorant

Phalacrocorax auritus

Beak

Flying

Feeding

Observation Calendar

J F M A M J J A S O N D

Male/Female: Overall black with long tail feathers; bright orange chin and throat patch; feet and legs black. Crest is visible only during courtship. In flight: neck is kinked.

Did you know? Cormorants are often seen perched on a rock or pier with wings fully extended to dry their feathers.

Often seen flying extremely high.

Voice: Call is a variety of grunts and croaks, only at its nest. Elsewhere silent.
Food: Small fish.
Nest/Eggs: Colonies. Platform built of sticks and twigs lined with leaves and grass, and placed on ground or small tree. 3-5 eggs.

Egg: Actual Size

19

Great Blue Heron
Ardea herodias

Size Identification

Beak

Flying

Feeding

Observation Calendar
J F M A M J J A S O N D

Male/Female: Overall grey-blue with black crest on top of head; long neck and bill; black patch around eyes and extending down long yellow bill; white head; long grey legs and feet; long feathers extend over wings and base of neck. In flight: neck is kinked; legs extend past tail; constant wing flapping with occasional glide.

Voice: Bill makes clacking sound. Call is a harsh *squawk*.
Food: Small fish, reptiles, amphibians, crustaceans, birds, aquatic insects.
Nest/Eggs: Colonies. Platform of aquatic plants and twigs lined with softer materials such as down and soft grass, placed in tree. 3-7 eggs.

Egg: Actual Size   20

Turkey Vulture
Cathartes aura

Observation Calendar
J F M A M J J A S O N D

Male/Female: Large overall black bird; silver-grey underside of wings is seen in flight; naked red head; pale yellow sharply curved beak; feet and legs charcoal.

Did you know? Turkey vultures are most commonly seen soaring high over the countryside with their long wings held upward in a wide V-shape.

Voice: Grunts and hisses during aggression or feeding.
Food: Carrion.
Nest/Eggs: Nest made of scrap on ground, usually in cave, on cliff, hollow of tree or in fallen log. 1-3 eggs.

Canada Goose

Branta canadensis

Size Identification

Beak

Flying

Observation Calendar
J F M A M J J A S O N D

Male/Female: Black head, neck and bill; white cheek patch; breast and belly pale brown with white flecks; feet and legs black; back and wings brown with white edging; short black tail; white rump, seen in flight. In flight: flies in "V" formations.

Feeding

Voice: Musical *honk*, repeated. Female has slightly higher pitched *honk*.
Food: Grass, various seeds and grains.
Nest/Eggs: Large nest of twigs, moss and grass lined with down feathers placed near water's edge. 4-8 eggs.

Egg: 75%

Mute Swan
Cygnus olor

Size Identification

Beak

Flying

Feeding

Observation Calendar

J F M A M J J A S O N D

Male/Female: White overall; bright orange or pink beak; black knob at base of beak; unique S-shaped neck when swimming; feet and legs black.

Did you know? The Mute Swan, native to Europe, was brought to North America in the nineteenth century as an ornamental species for parks and large estates.

Voice: Mostly silent. Occasional hissing and barking or loud trumpet call.
Food: Fresh and saltwater plants, algae, grains.
Nest/Eggs: Large pile of grass and moss lined with feathers, usually built on edge of pond or marsh. 4-6 eggs.

Egg: 45%

Size Identification

Beak

Flying

Feeding

Egg: 60%

Tundra Swan

Cygnus columbianus

Observation Calendar
J F M A M J J A S O N D

Male/Female: Overall white bird; black beak; yellow dash extending from eyes down to base of beak, but not always present; black facial area narrowing to eyes; neck and head occasionally appear lightly rusted colour; feet and legs black.

Voice: High-pitched whistling. Bugling sound; *hoo-ho-hoo* when migrating.
Food: Aquatic plants, mollusks, grains.
Nest/Eggs: Platform built of aquatic plants, grasses and moss on islands. 2-7 eggs.

Wood Duck

Aix sponsa

Observation Calendar
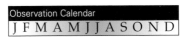

J F M A M J J A S O N D

Male: Green head and drooping crest; black cheeks; red eyes and white throat with two spurs; bill orange with black markings; chest brown with white spots leading to white belly; black and green back; sides tan with white and black band. In flight: long squared tail.

Female: Back and crown brown; white eye-ring; speckled breast and lighter coloured belly.

Voice: Male — high-pitched whistle. Female — loud *oooooeeek* in flight.

Food: Aquatic plants, insects, minnows, amphibians.

Nest/Eggs: In cavity of tree, as high as 20 metres, or in a log or built structure lined with wood chips and feathers. 9-12 eggs.

Egg: Actual Size

Gadwall
Anas strepera

Size Identification

Beak

Flying

Feeding

Observation Calendar

J F M A M J J A S O N D

Male: Body over all grey-brown; black rump and tail feathers; light grey pointed feathers on back; feet and legs orange; thin black banding over entire body; black bill.
Female: Dull greyish brown and black overall; black bill with orange on sides.

Voice: Quacking and high-pitched descending note from female. Male gives whistle and *rab rab* call.
Food: Seeds and aquatic plants.
Nest/Eggs: Nest built on islands from plant material and lined with down, slightly concealed. 7-13 eggs.

American Wigeon

Anas americana

Size Identification

Beak

Flying

Observation Calendar

J F M A M J J A S O N D

Male: White patch running up forehead from bill; green around eyes broadening at cheeks and descending on neck; brown changing to black on back and pointed wings; pointed tail feathers are black with white lines; bill white with black patches on top and on tip. In flight: green on trailing edge of wing; white forewing and belly.
Female: Overall light brown with brighter colour running down sides. No green patch on eyes.

Did you know? The American Wigeon is an opportunist: waiting for other diving ducks to come to the surface with their catch, they will attempt to steal the food.

Feeding

Voice: Male — occasional distinctive whistle: *wh-wh-whew.* Female quacks.
Food: Aquatic plants.
Nest/Eggs: Grasses lined with down, concealed under brush or tree, a distance from the water. 9-12 eggs.

Egg: 90%

American Black Duck
Anas rubripes

Size Identification

Beak

Flying

Feeding

Observation Calendar
J F M A M J J A S O N D

Male: Dark black with hint of brown overall and blue speculum; bill is olive; feet and legs orange. In flight: white patches at base of wings.
Female: Overall lighter brown than male with orange and black bill.

Voice: Both female and male *quack*. Male also whistles.
Food: Vegetation, insects, amphibians, snails, seeds, grains, berries.
Nest/Eggs: Depression on ground lined with grass, leaves and down, close to water's edge. 8-12 eggs.

Egg: Actual Size

Mallard

Anas platyrhynchos

Size Identification

Beak

Flying

Feeding

Observation Calendar

J F M A M J J A S O N D

Male: Bright green iridescent head, yellow bill; thin white collar; chestnut brown chest; grey sides; black and grey back; white tail; black curled feathers over rump; feet and legs orange. In flight: blue speculum with white border; underparts of wings grey and brown.
Female: Overall brown streaked with orange bill, black patches on bill; white tail feathers.

Voice: Male — call is a soft *raeb* repeated. Female — loud *quacks* repeated.
Food: Aquatic plants, grains, insects.
Nest/Eggs: Shallow cup built of grasses and aquatic plants lined with feathers on ground concealed near water. 8-10 eggs.

29

Egg: Actual Size

Blue-winged Teal

Anas discors

Size Identification

Beak

Flying

Feeding

Observation Calendar

J F M A M J J A S O N D

Male: Grey head with crescent shaped white patch running up face, black bill; brown chest and belly; back and wings dark brown with buff highlights; blue speculum; yellow feet and legs.

Female: Overall brown speckled with pale blue speculum.

Voice: Male has high-pitched *peeeep*. Female — *quack* is soft and high-pitched.

Food: Aquatic plants, seeds.

Nest/Eggs: Pile of grasses lined with down, close to waters edge, concealed. 9-12 eggs.

Egg: Actual Size

Northern Pintail

Anas acuta

Size Identification

Beak

Flying

Observation Calendar

J F M A M J J A S O N D

Feeding

Male: Brown head with white line circling around cheeks to chest; white chest and belly; back and wings are black and grey; long tail is black and brown; rump black; sides grey with thin black banding; bill grey with white line. In flight: long tail; white neck and line running up neck.
Female: Overall brown with black bill; less pintail feature.

Voice: Male has 2 high-pitched whistles. Female quacks.
Food: Aquatic plants, seeds, crustaceans, corn, grains.
Nest/Eggs: Bowl of sticks, twigs, grasses and lined with down at a distance from water's edge. 6-9 eggs.

31

Egg: 90%

Green-winged Teal
Anas crecca

Size Identification

Beak

Flying

Feeding

Egg: Actual Size

Observation Calendar

J F M A M J J A S O N D

Male: Head is rust with green patch running around eyes to back of head, black bill, black at back of base of neck; warm grey body with thin black banding; distinctive white bar running down side just in front of wing; white rump; short square tail.
Female: Overall dull brown with green speculum; dark band running through eyes.

Voice: Male — high-pitched whistle. Female — weak shrill voice.
Food: Seeds, aquatic plants, corn, wheat, oats.
Nest/Eggs: On ground, cup shaped, filled with grasses and weeds, sometimes a distance from water. 10-12 eggs.

Ring-necked Duck
Aythya collaris

Size Identification

Beak

Flying

Feeding

Observation Calendar
J F M A M J J A S O N D

Male: Back, head and breast black, high forehead; black bill with white outlines; yellow eyes; white spur on breast leading to grey underside and belly. In flight: grey trailing edge; white belly.

Female: Grey cheeks and bill; one white band at tip of bill; white eye-ring; dark charcoal back; brown chest, belly and sides.

Voice: Male has low, loud whistle. Female call is soft *prrrrrrrrr* notes. Mostly quiet.

Food: Aquatic plants, molluscs, insects.

Nest/Eggs: Cup shaped, built of grasses and moss and lined with down feathers, concealed near pond. 8-12 eggs.

33

Egg: 90%

Bufflehead
Bucephala albeola

Size Identification

Beak

Flying

Observation Calendar
J F M A M J J A S O N D

Male: Small compact duck; black head with large white patch behind each eye, grey bill; black back with white underparts.
Female: Grey-brown overall with smaller white patch behind each eye.

Voice: Mostly quiet. Male squeals. Female, low *prk prrk*.
Food: Small fish, crustaceans, molluscs and snails.

Feeding

Egg: Actual Size 34

Hooded Merganser
Lophodytes cucullatus

Beak

Flying

Feeding

Observation Calendar

J F M A M J J A S O N D

Male: Black crested head with large white patch on back of head behind each eye; black bill is long and thin; rust-coloured eyes; black back with rust sides and white underparts; black band runs down side into chest; white bands on black wings; tail is often cocked. In flight: rapid energetic wing beats.
Female: Grey breast and belly; faint rust colour on back of crest; wings dark brown.

Voice: Call is a low croaking or *gack*.
Food: Small fish, reptiles, crustaceans, molluscs and aquatic insects.
Nest/Eggs: In tree cavity or built structure lined with grasses and down feathers, occasionally on ground. 9-12 eggs.

Egg: Actual Size

Common Merganser
Mergus merganser

Size Identification

Beak

Flying

Observation Calendar

J F M A M J J A S O N D

Male: Dark green head crested with red toothed bill slightly hooked at end; white ring around neck connects to white chest and belly; black back and white sides; feet and legs orange.
Female: Brown head and grey-brown back; white chin.

Voice: Male call is *twaang*. Female call is series of hard notes.
Food: Small fish, crustaceans and molluscs.
Nest/Eggs: Built of reeds and grass and lined with down feathers in tree cavity, rock crevice, on ground or in built structure. 8-11 eggs.

Feeding

Egg: Actual Size   36

Ruddy Duck
Oxyura jamaicensis

Beak

Flying

Feeding

Observation Calendar

J F M A M J J A S O N D

Male: Distinct broad light blue bill; black cap running down back of neck; white cheeks; reddish-brown body; long black tail that is often held upright.
Female: Overall brown with white cheeks; buff line just below eyes; beak is black.

Voice: Mostly quiet except for drumming and clicking sounds by male during courting.
Food: Aquatic plants, crustaceans and aquatic insects.
Nest/Eggs: Floating nest of dry plant material lined with down and hidden amongst reeds. 6-20 eggs.

Egg: Actual Size

Osprey
Pandion haliaeetus

Size Identification

Beak

J F M A M J J A S O N D

Male/Female: In flight: white belly and chest; wings grey with black banding; white wing underparts connect to chest; black band running through eyes; large black bill; tail grey with black banding. Perched: black back and wings with thin white line running above wing; eyes yellow with black band running through and down to cheek; chin white; top of head white with black patches.

Female: Larger with a pronounced dark necklace.

Voice: A loud chirp that trails off, or ascending *squeeeee* during courtship displays.

Food: Various small fish.

Nest/Eggs: Constructed of twigs and sticks, lined with sod, grass and vines in upper parts of trees and on top of poles, 60 feet above ground. 2-3 eggs.

Nesting Location

Egg: 65%

Bald Eagle

Haliaeetus leucocephalus

Size Identification

Beak

Observation Calendar

J F M A M J J A S O N D

Male/Female: In flight: broad black wings and belly with white head and tail feathers. Perched: white head with brilliant yellow eyes, white tail feathers, black back and wings, yellow feet and legs; yellow bill.
Juvenile: Mistaken for Golden Eagle because it lacks white head and tail; chest, white and speckled; black wings with white speckles; underparts black with large areas of white.

Did you know? The eagle population is now recovering from rapid declines in the 1970s due to the widespread use of DDT and other insecticides.

Voice: A loud scream given in multiples.
Food: A variety of small and medium-sized mammals, fish and carrion.
Nest/Eggs: Upper parts of large, often dead, trees built with large twigs, lined with grass, moss, sod and weeds. 2 eggs.

Nesting Location

39

Egg: 70%

Size Identification

Beak

Backyard Feeder

Sharp-shinned Hawk
Accipiter striatus

Observation Calendar
J F M A M J J A S O N D

Male/Female: In flight: small hawk with rust-coloured chest banded with buff; long square tail is white with charcoal banding; wings dark brown and rounded; top of head dark brown. Perched: brick-red eyes with brown band just below eye; bill is black with yellow base; feet and legs yellow; white feathers extend out of rust-coloured belly.

Did you know? Over the past few years there has been a dramatic decrease in the eastern population. This may be directly related to the decrease in songbirds that it hunts.

Voice: A quick high-pitched *kik kik kik*.
Food: Small songbirds.
Nest/Eggs: Broad platforms of twigs and sticks in conifers or deciduous trees built against the trunk, lined with bark. 4-5 eggs.

Nesting Location

Egg: Actual Size   40

Red-tailed Hawk

Buteo jamaicensis

Size Identification

Beak

Observation Calendar

J F M A M J J A S O N D

Male/Female: In flight: Tail will appear faint red depending on light; broad wings and belly, white banded with charcoal. Perched: Wings are dark brown with buff edges; eyes brick red; bill yellow and black; feet and legs yellow with white feathers banded brown/charcoal to knees; tail brick red.

Voice: A scream that is a downward *keeer er er.*
Food: Small mammals, amphibians, nestlings, insects, reptiles and birds.
Nest/Eggs: Flat and shallow, stick and twig nest, lined with moss and evergreen sprigs, on rocky ledges or in trees that are in the open, 10-30 metres above ground. 2 eggs.

Nesting Location

41

Egg: 70%

Rough-legged Hawk
Buteo lagopus

Beak

Observation Calendar
J F M A M J J A S O N D

Male/Female: In-flight: Dark patches on white belly with banding; black patch at wrist of underwing; white tail with one dark band at tip. Perched: Dark brown wings with buff head that is banded with dark brown; yellow eyes; base of tail white rump; black bill, yellow at base; yellow feet and legs with buff feathers that are banded brown to knees.

Voice: A whistle along with a *keeeerrr* that descends.
Food: Small rodents.
Nest/Eggs: Stick nest in tree. 2-4 eggs

Nesting Location

Egg: 65%

American Kestrel

Falco sparverius

Size Identification

Beak

Observation Calendar
J F M A M J J A S O N D

Male/Female: In flight: overall buff with black speckles; distinctive black banding on face. Perched: blue-grey wings with black, separated banding; back rust with black banding; grey top of head with rust patch on top; black bands running down cheeks against white; bill black/charcoal with yellow at base; feet and legs orange; tail deep rust with broad black tip.

Voice: Rapid *klee klee klee* or *kily kily kily*.
Food: Mice, voles, insects and small birds.
Nest/Eggs: In cavity of tree or man-made boxes, little or no nesting material. 3-5 eggs.

Birdhouse Nester

Nesting Location

43

Egg: Actual Size

Peregrine Falcon
Falco peregrinus

Size Identification

Beak

Observation Calendar
J F M A M J J A S O N D

Male/Female: In flight: Overall white underside with charcoal banding; face has black mask and sideburns with yellow around dark eyes, bill is yellow and grey, feet and legs are yellow. Perched: Dark grey wings with buff edging on feathers.

Did you know? The Peregrine falcon has been introduced into large cities where they can nest on top of high-rise buildings.

Voice: A series of high-pitched screams — *ki ki ki*.
Food: Catches birds in flight and occasionally will eat larger insects.
Nest/Eggs: Slight hollow in rock ledge or flat roof top, built with sticks. 3-5 eggs.

Nesting Location

Egg: 70%

44

Ring-necked Pheasant

Phasianus colchicus

Observation Calendar

J F M A M J J A S O N D

Male: Green iridescent head with distinctive red wattles (patches around eyes), white collar, overall body is mixture of grey, black and brown; long tail feathers brown with black banding; feet and legs charcoal grey; pale yellow bill.
Female: Grey-brown overall with dark markers over entire body; pale yellow bill; small red wattle above eyes.

Did you know? This chicken-like bird gets into some real cock fights in early spring — jumping, pecking, clawing for their right to territory.

Voice: Loud, harsh *uurk-rk*.
Food: Seeds, insects, grains and berries.
Nest/Eggs: Shallow bowl on ground lined with weed, grass and leaves. 6-15 eggs.

Ruffed Grouse
Bonasa umbellus

Size Identification

Beak

Observation Calendar

J F M A M J J A S O N D

Male: Distinctive crest on head; overall brown speckled bird with black shoulder band on back of neck; tail is grey with broad black band at tip; eyes brown; feet and legs grey.
Female: Similar to male except browner and more barring on underside; black shoulder band is narrower.

Did you know? The female will act injured if there is a threat near the nest.

Voice: An alarm note of *qit qit*. Cooing by female. Male does drumming with wings like a distant motorboat.
Food: A variety of insects, seeds, tree buds, leaves and berries.
Nest/Eggs: Hollow under log or near the base of a tree lined with leaves, pine needles and feathers. 9-12 eggs.

Nesting Location

Egg: 90%   46

Wild Turkey

Meleagris gallopavo

Beak

Observation Calendar
J F M A M J J A S O N D

Male: An extremely large bird, overall dark dusky-brown body; iridescent bronze sheen and banding of reddish-brown, black and white; head is featherless, grey and red; blueish and reddish wattles; tail is fan shaped when open and has chestnut or buff tips; spurs and 'beard' on breast; feet and legs reddish-grey.

Female: Smaller than male and less iridescence; no spurs or 'beard.'

Voice: Gobbling and clucking calls.

Food: Seeds, grains, insects, frogs, lizards, vegetation and nuts.

Nest/Eggs: Scraped depression in ground lined with leaves and grasses. 6-20 eggs.

Nesting Location

47

Egg: 65%

Virginia Rail

Rallus limicola

Beak

Flying

Feeding

Observation Calendar
J F M A M J J A S O N D

Male/Female: Chicken-like; grey head banded dark charcoal on top; eyes red; neck and sides rich rust; long curved red and black bill; back dark brown with rust edging; wings rust with black; short brown tail; legs and feet red; belly black and white banding.

Voice: Call is a *kicket* repeated with grunting notes.
Food: Marine worms, snails, aquatic insects.
Nest/Eggs: Cup built of grass and reeds built slightly above water's surface attached to reeds and other aquatic plant life. 5-12 eggs.

Sora

Porzana carolina

Size Identification

Beak

Flying

Feeding

Observation Calendar

J F M A M J J A S O N D

Male/Female: Chicken-like; grey colouring above eyes runs down to chin, breast and belly; black mask behind thick yellow bill; upper parts chestnut brown with white and dark brown bars; legs and feet yellow.

Did you know? The Sora, like other rails, prefers to migrate at night.

Voice: Call is a musical *kuur weeee*, which is repeated and descends.
Food: Aquatic insects and seeds.
Nest/Eggs: Built in open marsh, attached to reeds, using leaves and grass. 6-15 eggs.

49

Egg: Actual Size

American Coot
Fulica americana

Observation Calendar

J F M A M J J A S O N D

Male/Female: Duck-like body, slate-coloured overall; white bill and frontal shield shows red swelling at close range; partial black ring around tip of beak; feet and legs greenish-yellow; lobed toes.

Did you know? The American Coot has many different courtship displays, including running over the surface of water with its neck and head bent very low.

Voice: Variety of calls including clucks, grunts and other harsh notes and toots sounding like a small trumpet.
Food: Seeds, leaves, roots and small aquatic plants.
Nest/Eggs: Floating platform nest of dead leaves and stems lined with finer material and anchored to reeds. 8-10 eggs.

Killdeer

Charadrius vociferus

Size Identification

Beak

Flying

Feeding

Observation Calendar

J F M A M J J A S O N D

Male/Female: Bright red eyes with black band running across forehead; white chin, collar and eyebrow; black collar ring under white; black chest band set against white chest and belly; back and wings rust and grey; wing tipped in black; legs and feet pink/grey. In flight: orange rump; black wing tips and white band through center.

Did you know? A Killdeer will exhibit a "broken-wing" display when a predator comes close to the nest site. The bird will appear hurt and run around distracting the predator from the nest.

Voice: Variety of calls with most common being *kill deeee*, which is repeated.
Food: Insects.
Nest/Eggs: Hollow on ground with some pebbles. Most popular sightings in gravel parking lots. 3-4 eggs.

Egg: Actual Size

Spotted Sandpiper
Actitis macularia

Observation Calendar

J F M A M J J A S O N D

Male/Female: *Summer*: Grey-brown on head, back and wings; white eyebrow and black line running from beak to back of neck; long orange bill; white chin, chest and belly with distinct charcoal spots; yellow feet and legs; bobbing tail.
Winter: White underparts — no spots. In flight: quick stiff wingbeats, slightly arched back.

Voice: Quiet bird but makes a *peeetaawet* call during courtship and a whistle that is repeated when alarmed.
Food: Insects, worms, crustaceans, fish, flies and beetles.
Nest/Eggs: Shallow depression on ground lined with grasses and mosses. 4 eggs.

Ring-billed Gull
Larus delawarensis

Beak

Flying

Observation Calendar

J F M A M J J A S O N D

Male/Female: *Summer*: White overall; yellow bill with black band at end; yellow eyes; pale grey wings and black tips and white patches within black tips; yellow feet and legs. *Winter*: Feet and legs turn paler; light brown spots on top of head and back of neck. In flight: grey underparts; black wing tips.

Voice: Loud *kaawk* and other calls.
Food: Dives for fish, also eats insects, bird eggs, worms, garbage.
Nest/Eggs: Colonies. Grasses, sticks, twigs and pebbles built on ground. 3 eggs.

Feeding

53

Egg: Actual Size

Herring Gull
Larus argentatus

Size Identification

Beak

Flying

Feeding

Observation Calendar
J F M A M J J A S O N D

Male/Female: White head that in winter is streaked light brown; yellow eyes and bill; small red patch on lower bill; tail black; feet and legs pink. In flight: grey wing with white on trailing edge and black tips; pale brown rump; wide charcoal tail feathers.

Voice: Variety of squawks and squeals. Aggressive alarm call is *kak kak kak kak* ending in *yucca*.
Food: Insects, small mammals, clams, fish, small birds, crustaceans, mussels, rodents, garbage.
Nest/Eggs: Colonies. Mound lined with grass and seaweed on ground or cliff. Usually on islands. 2-4 eggs.

Great Black-backed Gull

Larus marinus

Size Identification

Beak

Flying

Feeding

Observation Calendar
J F M A M J J A S O N D

Male/Female: White head, chin, chest and belly, red patch on lower portion of bill; feet and legs pink/grey; black wings with thin white band on trailing edge; tail and back black. In flight: pale grey undersides with black wing tip; tail white.

Voice: Loud squawks and deep guttural notes.
Food: Scavenger. Small fish, mammals, young birds and garbage. Major predator of other birds including puffin and tern chicks.
Nest/Eggs: Colonies. Mound of seaweed and other coastal plants lined with grasses on ground or rocky ledge. 3 eggs.

Egg: 80%

Rock Dove (Pigeon)
Columba livia

Observation Calendar
J F M A M J J A S O N D

Male/Female: Varies greatly from solid white to solid black and everything in between. Most birds have dark grey head with hints of iridescent colours along the neck; body light grey with two charcoal wing bands; tail and wings dark grey with black bands; rump is white.

Did you know? Pigeons were introduced to North America in the 1800s. They are now common everywhere, especially in urban areas.

Voice: Soft descending *kooooo kooooo*.
Food: Seeds and grains.
Nest/Eggs: Flimsy nest of twigs, grass, straw and debris, on ledges or crevices of buildings and bridges, in colonies. 1-2 eggs.

Mourning Dove

Zenaida macroura

Size Identification

Beak

Backyard Feeder

Observation Calendar

J F M A M J J A S O N D

Male: Buff-coloured head and body; dark grey wings and tail; bill is black with speckles of red at opening; wings have small black feathers highlighted against softer grey; eyes black surrounded by light blue; feet and legs red; tail is long and pointed.
Female: Similar except for head, neck and chest, which are evenly brown.

Did you know? When the Mourning Dove is in flight its wings whistle.

Voice: Very distinct cooing that sounds a little sad, *coooahooo-oo -oo-oo* fading at the end.
Food: A variety of seeds and grains.
Nest/Eggs: Platform of sticks and twigs, lined with grass and rootlets, in evergreens, up to 15 metres above ground. 1-2 eggs.

Nesting Location

Egg: Actual Size

Black-billed Cuckoo
Coccyzus erythropthalmus

Size Identification

Beak

Observation Calendar
J F M A M J J A S O N D

Male/Female: Distinct black beak curved slightly downward; red ring around black eyes; upper body parts brown; wings brown; long tail with 3 white spots on underside; white chin, chest and belly; feet and legs charcoal grey.

Did you know? The Black-billed Cuckoo is an important species for farmers since much of its diet consists of caterpillars, which are destructive to plants.

Nesting Location

Voice: Softly repeated *cu cu cu cu cu* in groups of 2-5 at the same pitch.
Food: Insects, lizards, mollusks, fishes, frogs and berries.
Nest/Eggs: Shallow, built of twigs and grasses and lined with softer materials including ferns, roots and plant-down; usually built near tree trunk in dense area. 2-5 eggs.

Egg: Actual Size

Yellow-billed Cuckoo

Coccyzus americanus

Observation Calendar
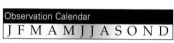
J F M A M J J A S O N D

Male/Female: Overall brownish grey on upper parts; long curved black beak with yellow below; long black tail with 3 white ovals on underside; white chin, chest and belly; feet and legs black.

Voice: Call is a rapid *ka ka ka ka kow kow kowp kowp,* slowing down at end.

Food: Hairy caterpillar and other insects, berries, frogs and lizards.

Nest/Eggs: Flimsy saucer built of twigs and lined with leaves and grasses, built in bushes or small trees. 1-4 eggs.

Eastern Screech-Owl
Otus asio

Size Identification

Beak

Birdhouse Nester

Nesting Location

Egg: Actual Size

Observation Calendar
J F M A M J J A S O N D

Male/Female: Small reddish or brown-grey owl with mottling of dark brown; large yellow eyes; feet and legs pale; small black curved beak; reddish ear tufts. Also occurs in grey morph with grey intermediates.

Voice: Call is high-pitched rising and lowering with long trill. Soft purring and trills.
Food: Mice, insects, amphibians, small birds.
Nest/Eggs: Tree cavity with no lining added. 3-6 eggs.

Great Horned Owl

Bubo virginianus

Size Identification

Beak

Observation Calendar

J F M A M J J A S O N D

Male/Female: Very recognizable ear tufts that sit wide apart; bright yellow eyes surrounded by rust colour; grey and brown overall with black bands.

Voice: Hoot consists of *hoo hoo hoo hoo hoo hoo*.
Food: Small mammals, birds and reptiles.
Nest/Eggs: Nests in a deserted hawk's, heron's or crow's nest with very little material added. Occasionally will lay eggs on ground amongst bones, skulls and bits of fur. 1-3 eggs.

Nesting Location

Egg: 70%

Chimney Swift
Chaetura pelagica

Observation Calendar

J F M A M J J A S O N D

Male/Female: Dark charcoal on head, back, wings and tail; lighter on chest and throat; black bill is small with light grey on underside; feet and legs grey.

Did you know? A Chimney Swift is capable of snapping off tree twigs with its feet while in flight. It then takes the twig in its mouth and returns to its nest.

Voice: A very quick and repeated *chitter, chitter, chitter* with occasional *chip*.
Food: Flying insects such as moths and beetles.
Nest/Eggs: Flimsy half-cup attached by saliva to crevice or ledge in chimneys, barns and old buildings, and on rock formations. 3-6 eggs.

Ruby-throated Hummingbird

Archilochus colubris

Beak

Backyard Feeder

Observation Calendar
J F M A M J J A S O N D

Male: Dark green head that is iridescent in parts; red throat, darker under chin; white collar, breast and belly; wings and notched tail black; iridescent green on back; black bill is long and thin; feet and legs black.

Female: Head, back and parts of tail are bright iridescent green; white throat, chest and belly; wings and tail black with white outer tips; black bill is long and thin; small white area behind eyes; feet and legs black.

Voice: A low *hummmmmm* produced by wings. Occasionally an angry sounding squeak or chattering.

Food: Nectar from a variety of plants including thistles, jewelweed, trumpet vines and other blossoms; occasionally insects.

Nest/Eggs: Thimble-sized, tightly woven cup with deep cavity built with fibres and attached with spiderweb, lined with plant down, covered on the outside with lichens, in tree or shrub, 3-6 metres above ground. 2 eggs.

Nesting Location

63

Belted Kingfisher

Ceryle alcyon

Size Identification

Beak

Flying

Feeding

Observation Calendar
J F M A M J J A S O N D

Male: A large crested blue/black head and long black bill; wings black with white bands; chest white; white collar wraps around neck with blue band that wraps around chest; very short blue tail; feet and legs charcoal.
Female: Rust-coloured breast band.

Did you know? Belted Kingfishers teach their young to dive for food by catching a fish, stunning it, then placing it on the surface of the water. The young birds then practice diving for it.

Voice: A continuous deep rattle during flight.
Food: Small fish, amphibians, reptiles, insects and crayfish.
Nest/Eggs: A cavity or tunnel excavated in a bank near a river or lake. 5-8 eggs.

Egg: Actual Size   64

Red-headed Woodpecker

Melanerpes erythrocephalus

Beak

Backyard Feeder

Observation Calendar

J F M A M J J A S O N D

Male/Female: Bright red hood over head with grey and black bill; back is black with large distinctive white patches on wings; feet and legs grey; tail feathers are pointed and black; chest and belly white.

Did you know? These woodpeckers are declining because of forestry practices and are competing unsuccessfully with European Starlings for nesting locations.

Voice: Call is a deep hoarse *queer queeeer queeer*.
Food: A variety of insects and insect larvae.
Nest/Eggs: Cavity of tree with no added material, 2-25 metres above ground. 4-7 eggs.

Nesting Location

Egg: Actual Size

Beak

Backyard Feeder

Birdhouse Nester

Nesting Location

Red-bellied Woodpecker

Melanerpes carolinus

Observation Calendar
J F M A M J J A S O N D

Male: Bright red cap stretching down back of neck; long sharp black beak; tan chin, chest and belly; short black tail with white stripes; black back with white bands; feet and legs charcoal grey; reddish patch on lower belly seldom visible.
Female: Grey face with red crown running down back of head.

Did you know? The Red-bellied Woodpecker will store food in tree cavities and crevices.

Voice: Harsh *churrrr* and *chuck chuck chuck* descending in pitch. Drums and bursts.
Food: Insects, fruit, seeds and nuts.
Nest/Eggs: Creates cavity in living or nearly dead tree. 3-8 eggs.

Downy Woodpecker

Picoides pubescens

Size Identification

Beak

Backyard Feeder

Birdhouse Nester

Nesting Location

Observation Calendar
J F M A M J J A S O N D

Male: Black crown ends in very bright red spot on back of head; white extends from cheeks to lower belly; wings and tail black with white banding; feet and legs grey.
Female: Similar except without red spot on back of head.

Voice: A bright sounding *peek...peek,* which may be followed by a rattling call. Listen for bird pounding on trees looking for insects.
Food: Larvae and other tree-dwelling insects.
Nest/Eggs: Cavity of tree with no added material, 1-5 metres above ground. 3-6 eggs.

Egg: Actual Size

Hairy Woodpecker
Picoides villosus

Size Identification

Beak

Backyard Feeder

Nesting Location

Egg: Actual Size

Observation Calendar
J F M A M J J A S O N D

Male: Black crown ending in bright red spot on back of head; white extends from cheeks to lower belly; black wings and tail with white banding; black feet and legs; black bill is lightly covered with feathers. The bill on the Hairy Woodpecker is slightly longer than the Downy Woodpecker's.
Female: Similar except without red spot on back of head.

Did you know? An easy way to identify Downy and Hairy Woodpeckers is that they both spread their tails when perched against the side of a tree.

Voice: Hairy Woodpeckers make various sounds as they pound on trees. One sound is for hole digging while another is when it is looking for food.
Food: Larvae and other tree-dwelling insects, fruits, ants and corn.
Nest/Eggs: Cavity of tree with no added material, up to 10 metres above ground. 3-6 eggs.

Northern Flicker

Colaptes auratus

Beak

Backyard Feeder

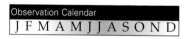

Observation Calendar

J F M A M J J A S O N D

Male: Grey at top of head, which stops at bright red spot on back of neck; black eyes are encircled in light brown, with a black line running off bill to lower neck; chest begins with black half-moon necklace on front and turns into a white belly with black spots; wings and tail greyish-brown with black banding; white rump; yellow feathers are evident under sharp pointed tail feathers while in flight.

Female: Similar to male except without the black line running from bill.

Voice: Various sounds depending on its use. When claiming its territory, a series of *kekekekeke*, and when in courtship, *woeka-woeka-woeka*.

Food: Digs and pokes on the ground looking for ants and other insects, fruit and seeds. Most of its diet consists of ants.

Nest/Eggs: Cavity of tree with no added material, up to 18 metres above ground. 3-10 eggs.

Nesting Location

Egg: Actual Size

Size Identification

Beak

Eastern Wood-Pewee
Contopus virens

Observation Calendar

J F M A M J J A S O N D

Male/Female: Olive-grey overall with head that is crested at back; wings black and dark grey with two white bars; throat and chest white; belly slightly yellow or white; tail charcoal; bill black on top and yellow underside; feet and legs black.

Did you know? The Wood-Pewee changes its voice in morning and evening, converting its song into a slow verse.

Voice: A soft whistle, *pee-a-wee pee-awee*, repeated without any pause early in the morning.

Food: Flies, beetles, bees, ants and other insects.

Nest/Eggs: Shallow cup built with grass, spiderweb and fibres lined with hair, covered outside with lichens, on horizontal branch of tree far out from trunk, 5-20 metres above ground. 3-5 eggs.

Nesting Location

Egg: Actual Size

Least Flycatcher

Empidonax minimus

Size Identification

Beak

Observation Calendar

J F M A M J J A S O N D

Male/Female: Smallest of the flycatchers with a brown/olive head and back; rump is slightly golden; throat white and washes to a grey breast and a pale yellow belly; black eyes are ringed with white; wings dark brown and black with white wing bands; tail dark olive/brown with white edges.

Did you know? The Least Flycatcher is not afraid of humans, and when it is in pursuit of a flying insect it will dive very close to a person.

Voice: Song is *chibic chibic chibic* repeated with accent in middle of phrase.
Food: Flying insects.
Nest/Eggs: Compact and deep cup built with bark, weeds, grasses and lined with thistle, feathers, hair and fibres, in upright fork of tree or shrub, 1-20 metres above ground. 3-6 eggs.

Nesting Location

Egg: Actual Size

Eastern Phoebe
Sayornis phoebe

Observation Calendar
J F M A M J J A S O N D

Male/Female: Grey-brown head and back with white throat and chest; feet and legs black; white wing bands; pale yellow belly.

Did you know? One quick way to identify this bird is to watch the greyish brown tail bobbing up and down.

Nesting Location

Voice: Song is a rough-sounding *fee bee fee bee*. Call is *wit*.
Food: Flying insects as well as ground insects.
Nest/Eggs: Large shelf structure built with weeds, grass, fibres and mud, covered with moss, lined with grass and hair. 3-6 eggs.

Great Crested Flycatcher

Myiarchus crinitus

Observation Calendar

J F M A M J J A S O N D

Male/Female: Olive/grey head with crest; back is olive/grey; wings are black with olive/grey edges and rust colour on outer edge; tail strong reddish-brown; throat soft grey changing to pale yellow at belly; feet and legs black.

Did you know? The Great Crested Flycatcher will sometimes use foil or cellophane in its nest.

Voice: A throaty whistle *wheeep* or a rolling *prrrreeeet*.
Food: Flying insects and a variety of ground insects.
Nest/Eggs: Bulky cup built with twig, leaves, feather, bark and cast off snakeskin, or cellophane, in natural cavity of tree, up to 18 metres above ground. 4-8 eggs.

Birdhouse Nester

Nesting Location

73

Egg: Actual Size

Eastern Kingbird

Tyrannus tyrannus

Size Identification

Beak

Observation Calendar
J F M A M J J A S O N D

Male/Female: Black head, back, wings and tail; white chin, chest and belly; wings have white along edge and tail has white band along tip; feet and legs black.

Did you know? Size does not matter to the Eastern Kingbird: they will attack crows, ravens, hawks and owls to defend their territory.

Voice: Several different calls, including *tzi tzee* as a true song. Also a *kitter kitter kitter* when threatened.
Food: Flying insects, and fruit in late summer.
Nest/Eggs: Bulky cup built with weed stalks, grass and moss, in branches of tree or shrub, 3-6 metres above ground. 3-5 eggs.

Nesting Location

Egg: Actual Size   74

Warbling Vireo

Vireo gilvus

Beak

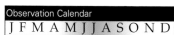

Observation Calendar
J F M A M J J A S O N D

Male/Female: Grey and green head, neck and back; white eyebrow extending from black bill; white chin, breast and belly with variable amounts of yellow; feet and legs black; tail and wings slightly darker.

Voice: The best way to find a Warbling Vireo is to listen. This bird sings throughout the day with a beautiful warbling sound. Song is group of slurred phrases such as *brig-a-dier brig-a-dier brigate*.

Food: Small insects including caterpillars, beetles and moths, and some berries.

Nest/Eggs: Tightly woven pensile cup built with bark, leaves, grass, feathers, plant down and spiderweb, lined with stems and horsehair, suspended in tall trees at the edge of wooded area, well away from trunk. 3-5 eggs.

Nesting Location

75 Egg: Actual Size

Red-eyed Vireo
Vireo olivaceus

Size Identification

Beak

Observation Calendar
J F M A M J J A S O N D

Male/Female: *Spring:* red eyes encircled with thin line of black set against a wide white eyebrow that runs from bill to back of head; black bill; throat and chest white; feet and legs black; back and rump are olive green; wings and tail black with edges of olive green; eyes are darker brown in winter.

Voice: The Red-eyed Vireo may sound over 40 different phrases in just 60 seconds, then begin all over again. A variety of short phrases including *cherrrwit chereeee cissy a witt teeeooo.*
Food: Small insects, berries and fruit.
Nest/Eggs: Deep cup built with grass, paper, bark, rootlets, vine and decorated outside with spiderweb and lichen, suspended in branches, up to 18 metres above ground; 4 eggs.

Nesting Location

Egg: Actual Size

Blue Jay

Cyanocitta cristata

Size Identification

Beak

Backyard Feeder

Nesting Location

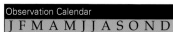

Observation Calendar

J F M A M J J A S O N D

Male/Female: Bright blue crested head with black band running through eyes to just under crest on back of neck; black band continues along side of neck on both sides to chest; white under chin; back is blue; wings and tail are blue banded with black and tipped with white at ends; black bill is large with light feathers covering nostril area; feet and legs black.

Did you know? The Blue Jay has a bad reputation for eating the eggs of other birds, and even their young.

Voice: Call is *jay jay jay*, plus many other calls including mimicking hawks.

Food: Omnivorous — in summer months the Blue Jay feasts on just about anything, including spiders, snails, salamanders, frogs, seeds and caterpillars. In winter months they supplement their diet with acorns and other nuts stored in tree cavities earlier in the year.

Nest/Eggs: Bulky nest of sticks, leaves, string and moss lined with small roots, well hidden, 1-15 metres above ground, in tree or shrub. 4-5 eggs.

Egg: Actual Size

American Crow
Corvus brachyrhynchos

Observation Calendar
J F M A M J J A S O N D

Male/Female: Overall shiny black with a hint of purple in direct sunlight; large broad black bill; short and slightly square tail; feet and legs black.

Did you know? Although one might think that crows are a nuisance bird, they actually devour large quantities of grasshoppers, beetles and grubs that can be destructive to crops.

Voice: A variety of calls. Most common is the long *caaaaaw*, which softens at the end.
Food: Omnivorous — insects, food waste, grains, seeds and carrion.
Nest/Eggs: Large basket of twigs, sticks, vines, moss, feathers, fur and hair, on ledge in crotch of tree or shrub. 3-4 eggs.

Horned Lark

Eremophila alpestris

Size Identification

Beak

Observation Calendar
J F M A M J J A S O N D

Male/Female: Dull brown on top; chest and belly white; wings and tail brown and black; distinctive black facial marks, which include small horns (feathers) on either side of its head; chin pale yellow with black band above running through eyes and down; feet and legs black.

Did you know? The horns are not always visible, but a quick way to identify the Horned Lark is that on the ground it walks and does not hop, like most small birds.

Voice: Soft twittering *tsee titi* or *zzeeet*.
Food: A variety of insects, seeds and grains.
Nest/Eggs: Hollow in ground under grass tuft, made of stems and leaves, lined with grass. 3-5 eggs.

Nesting Location

Egg: Actual Size

Purple Martin

Progne subis

Observation Calendar
J F M A M J J A S O N D

Male: Very shiny, dark purple overall, with black wings and tail; black bill is short and slightly curved; feet and legs reddish black; wings very long reaching to tip of tail when folded.

Female: Dull purple head and back with black wings and tail; chest and chin grey; belly white with black speckles; feet and legs black.

Voice: Call is a high-pitched *cheer cheer*.
Food: Flying insects.
Nest/Eggs: Deep cup in tree cavity lined with grass and leaves, usually in large colonies. Also nests in gourds and special martin houses. 3-8 eggs.

Tree Swallow

Tachycineta bicolor

Beak

Observation Calendar
J F M A M J J A S O N D

Male/Female: Dark iridescent blue on head, neck, back, wings and tail; bright white chin, chest and belly; black bill is short and slightly curved; wings are very long reaching down to tip of tail when folded; feet and legs charcoal.

Did you know? The Tree Swallow is the only swallow that eats berries in the place of insects. This allows it to winter further north than its relatives.

Voice: Early morning song *wheet trit weet*, with an alarm call of *cheedeeep*.
Food: Flying insects and berries.
Nest/Eggs: Cup in cavity of tree lined with grass and feathers, usually a woodpecker's old hole. 4-6 eggs.

Birdhouse Nester

Nesting Location

81

Egg: Actual Size

Size Identification

Beak

Northern Rough-winged Swallow
Stelgidopteryx serripennis

Male/Female: Greyish pale brown upper parts; pale brown chin, chest and sides; white belly; feet and legs black; short black beak; short tail.

Voice: Harsh *brrrrrt* during aggression or danger. Musical *br rrrrt* drawn out and often doubled.
Food: Insects in flight.
Nest/Eggs: Built in cavities such as tunnels, bridges, culverts and caves, lined with grass, leaves and moss. 4-8 eggs.

Nesting Location

Bank Swallow

Riparia riparia

Beak

Observation Calendar

J F M A M J J A S O N D

Male/Female: Dirty brown overall with white front except for brown band running across chest; wings are very long, reaching down to tip of tail when folded; feet and legs grey; black bill is short.

Voice: A variety of calls including *tchirrt tchirrt* and long twittering.

Food: Flying insects as well as a variety of other insects. Main diet consists of dragonflies, flies, mayflies and beetles.

Nest/Eggs: Earth tunnel lined with grass and straw along bank near water. 4-6 eggs.

Nesting Location

Egg: Actual Size

Cliff Swallow

Petrochelidon pyrrhonota

Size Identification

Beak

Observation Calendar

J F M A M J J A S O N D

Male/Female: Dark grey back and wings with buff rump and brick red cheeks; white patch on forehead; belly white; back has variable amounts of white streaks; feet and legs grey; tail black, square at end.

Did you know? Nest sites can be a little competitive and the birds will steal nesting grasses and twigs from each other's nests.

Nesting Location

Voice: A long *chuuurrrr* and a deeper *nyeeew.*
Food: A variety of insects.
Nest/Eggs: Mud lined with grass, hair and feathers, under bridges, in cliffs and buildings. 3-6 eggs.

Barn Swallow

Hirundo rustica

Size Identification

Beak

Observation Calendar

J F M A M J J A S O N D

Male: Dark blue iridescent from top of head, shoulders, down back and top of wings; chin and chest rust colour; wings are very long and extend to tips of tail, which is forked with long outer feathers that can be seen when bird is in flight; feet and legs charcoal; black and cream bill. When bird is in flight a band of white can be seen at end of tail.
Female: Same markings but duller.

Did you know? Barn Swallows are amazing to watch as they skim over water and pick insects off the surface. In the evening they hunt mosquitoes.

Voice: A soft twittering *kvik kvik wit wit.*
Food: A variety of insects.
Nest/Eggs: Mud and straw lined with feathers, in buildings, under bridges, in cliffs and caves. 4-5 eggs.

Nesting Location

85

Egg: Actual Size

Beak

Backyard Feeder

Birdhouse Nester

Nesting Location

Black-capped Chickadee

Poecile atricapilla

Observation Calendar

J F M A M J J A S O N D

Male/Female: Round black head with white cheeks; black chin that contrasts against bright white breast, which fades into rust on belly with buff edges; wings black and grey with white edges; tail black with white edges; feet and legs black.

Did you know? In winter Black-capped Chickadees form small flocks of about 10 birds and defend their territory from intruders.

Voice: A descending whistle with two notes and sounds like *chick-a-dee-dee-dee*.
Food: Seeds, insects and berries. Drawn to thistle-seed feeders.
Nest/Eggs: Domed cup lined with wool, hair, fur, moss and insect cocoons, in cavity of tree. 5-10 eggs.

Red-breasted Nuthatch

Sitta canadensis

Size Identification

Beak

Backyard Feeder

Birdhouse Nester

Nesting Location

Observation Calendar

J F M A M J J A S O N D

Male: Small round bird with black stripe over top of head and white stripe underneath, followed by black band running through eyes; white cheeks turn to rust colour at neck and continue rust to chest and belly; back is grey-blue; wings and tail grey becoming black at ends; black bill is often white on underside; feet and legs brown-black.

Female: Similar to male except for grey cap and light underside.

Did you know? The Red-breasted Nuthatch will smear pitch at the entrance to its nest, although it is not known why.

Voice: A tin-whistle call and an occasional loud *knack knack*.

Food: Seeds, insects and flying insects.

Nest/Eggs: Cup lined with grass, moss and feathers, in excavated cavity or crevice of tree. 1-12 metres above ground. 4-7 eggs.

Egg: Actual Size

White-breasted Nuthatch

Sitta carolinensis

Size Identification

Beak

Backyard Feeder

Birdhouse Nester

Nesting Location

Observation Calendar
J F M A M J J A S O N D

Male: Shiny black on top of head running down the back, turning to lighter blue-grey on back; white face and neck, chest and belly; slight rust colours on sides; wings and tail are blue-grey with white edges; feet and legs black.
Female: Similar to male except top of head and back are lighter grey.

Did you know? These little birds are known for their ability to run down tree trunks headfirst, at a very fast pace.

Voice: Nesting pairs keep in contact with one another with a deep sounding *aank aank* but also chatter a soft *ip ip*.
Food: Spiders, insects, seeds, insect eggs and acorns.
Nest/Eggs: Cup lined with twig, feathers, small roots, fur and hair, in natural cavity or crevice of tree, 4-15 metres above ground. 5-10 eggs.

Egg: Actual Size

Brown Creeper
Certhia americana

Size Identification

Beak

Backyard Feeder

Nesting Location

Egg: Actual Size

Observation Calendar
J F M A M J J A S O N D

Male/Female: Overall brown with grey streaks and white chin, chest and belly; long curved bill that is black on top and white/pink on bottom; distinctive eye stripe; feet and legs grey; tail is long and pointed.

Did you know? Spending most of its day creeping up and down trees looking for meals, the Brown Creeper can flatten itself and blend into the colour of the tree trunk when a predator passes by.

Voice: A very high whistling *see wee see tu eee.*
Food: Insects, insect and spider eggs and occasionally nuts and seeds.
Nest/Eggs: Cup with foundation of twig, bark and leaves, lined with bark, grass, feathers and moss, in cavity or under loose bark of tree, up to 5 metres above ground. 4-8 eggs.

House Wren
Troglodytes aedon

Size Identification

Beak

Birdhouse Nester

Observation Calendar
J F M A M J J A S O N D

Male/Female: Brown upper parts; light buff eyebrows; short rust and black banded tail that is often cocked; light buff chin, chest and belly; light buff banding along sides; feet and legs greyish pink; sharp black beak with yellow lower mandible.

Voice: Warbling that descends for 2-3 seconds. Call is a variety of buzzes and rattling *chur*.
Food: Insects.
Nest/Eggs: In cavities of trees or birdhouses, twigs lined with softer material including moss, feathers, rootlets and grasses. 5-6 eggs.

Nesting Location

Egg: Actual Size

Golden-crowned Kinglet

Regulus satrapa

Observation Calendar

J F M A M J J A S O N D

Male: One of the smallest woodland birds with black head stripes that set off its crown patch of orange; neck and back olive-grey; wings and tail olive with black along edges; feet and legs black; pale grey wingbars; pale eyebrow.
Female: Similar to male except patch on top is yellow.

Did you know? Their movements on a tree make them easy to spot. They flutter their wings as they look for insects.

Voice: Very high pitched, dropping to a quick chatter. The song is so highly pitched that some people cannot hear its song.
Food: A variety of insects, spiders, fruits and seeds.
Nest/Eggs: Deep cup built with moss and lichen at top, lined with black rootlets and feathers suspended from conifer branch, up to 30 metres above ground. 5-11 eggs.

Ruby-crowned Kinglet

Regulus calendula

Size Identification

Beak

Observation Calendar

J F M A M J J A S O N D

Male: Olive-grey overall with white eye-ring broken at top; crested with red patch on head; chin and neck are lighter olive-grey; feet and legs black; wings and tail buff with black edges; white bands on wings.
Female: Similar to male except for no red patch on top of head.

Did you know? The ruby red top on the male is hard to see unless he is courting, when it will flare up.

Nesting Location

Voice: High-pitched *tee tee tee* followed by a lower *tew tew tew* and ending with a chatter.
Food: Insects, insect eggs, spiders, fruits and seeds.
Nest/Eggs: Deep woven cup built with moss, lichen at top and lined with small black roots and feathers, suspended from conifer branch. 5-10 eggs.

Eastern Bluebird

Sialia sialis

Size Identification

Beak

Backyard Feeder

Birdhouse Nester

Nesting Location

Observation Calendar

J F M A M J J A S O N D

Male: Bright blue upper parts; tan throat and sides; white belly; feet and legs black.

Female: Similar to male except paler and head has greyish spotting.

Voice: Song is bright whistle *cheer cheerful charmer*. Call is lower *turrweee*.

Food: Variety of insects. Visits feeders for peanut butter, berries, mealworm or raisins.

Nest/Eggs: Built in cavity of tree or birdhouse from a variety of grasses and pine needles, lined with softer material. 3-6 eggs.

93

Egg: Actual Size

Veery

Catharus fuscescens

Size Identification

Beak

Observation Calendar
J F M A M J J A S O N D

Male/Female: Overall reddish-brown upper parts; white buff chest and belly; soft tan spotting along chin and cheeks; grey sides; feet and legs pinkish-grey.

Voice: Soft descending notes — *turreeooreooo-reeoorreeo*. Call is a loud descending *veerr*.
Food: Various insects, larvae, snails, earthworms, spiders and wild berries.
Nest/Eggs: Built of stems, twigs and mosses lined with softer material including various grasses and rootlets. 3-5 eggs.

Nesting Location

Wood Thrush

Hylocichla mustelina

Observation Calendar

J F M A M J J A S O N D

Male/Female: Rust-coloured head fades to a brown back; wings and tail dark brown with black ends; feet and legs grey with pink; white eye-ring; chin and chest white with black spotting, underparts grey.

Voice: Suggestive of a flute, the song is a series of varied phrases — *ee oh lee ee oh lay.*

Food: A variety of insects on the ground and in trees.

Nest/Eggs: Firm and compact cup built with grass, paper, moss, bark and mud, lined with small roots in tree or shrub, 2-15 metres above ground. 3-4 eggs.

American Robin

Turdus migratorius

Size Identification

Beak

Backyard Feeder

Observation Calendar
J F M A M J J A S O N D

Male: Charcoal/brown head with distinctive white above and below eyes; back and wings charcoal brown with white edges; tail dark grey; throat dark grey with thin white banding; chest and belly brick red; feet and legs black; bill yellow.
Female: Breast is slightly paler than male's.

Voice: Song is *cheerily cheerily cheerily* in a whistle tone.
Food: Earthworms, insects and fruit.
Nest/Eggs: Deep cup built with weed stalks, cloth, string and mud, lined with grass, in evergreens and deciduous trees or shrubs. 4 eggs.

Nesting Location

Egg: Actual Size

Gray Catbird
Dumetella carolinensis

Size Identification

Beak

Observation Calendar

J F M A M J J A S O N D

Male/Female: Distinctive black cap with overall grey body; brick red under tail, which is hidden most of the time; feet and legs grey with hints of pink.

Did you know? Catbirds actually migrate during the night hours and research indicates they use the moon for navigating.

Voice: A distinctive cat-like *meeow* and *kwut*.
Food: A variety of insects, spiders and wild berries.
Nest/Eggs: Bulky deep cup built with twigs, vines, grass, paper and weeds lined with small roots, in dense thickets of tree or shrub, 1-3 metres above ground. 3-6 eggs.

Nesting Location

Egg: Actual Size

Brown Thrasher
Toxostoma rufum

Size Identification

Beak

Nesting Location

J F M A M J J A S O N D

Male/Female: Distinctive long black bill; grey chin, white chest and belly streaked with dark brown; long reddish-brown tail and back; reddish-brown crown on head; feet and legs pinkish-grey; white and black banding on wings.

Voice: Call is a loud *smack*. Voice mimics other birds and is usually repeated twice.
Food: Variety of insects, frogs, lizards, snakes and various wild berries.
Nest/Eggs: Built of twigs, sticks and dead leaves lined with softer material including grasses and rootlets. 2-6 eggs.

Egg: Actual Size 98

European Starling

Sturnus vulgaris

Size Identification

Beak

Backyard Feeder

Birdhouse Nester

Nesting Location

Observation Calendar

J F M A M J J A S O N D

Male/Female: *Summer:* Black iridescent bird with light white speckles over entire body; bill is sharp yellow; wing and tail are edged in white and brown; feet and legs are red. *Winter:* Speckles increase and some become brown; bill is black; feet and legs are red; wings and tail have more brown.

Did you know? Sixty starlings were introduced into New York City in 1890. Since then they have spread throughout North America.

Voice: Mimics the songs of other birds and even sounds of cats and whistles.
Food: A variety of insects including worms and grubs, and weed seeds.
Nest/Eggs: Loose cup in cavity filled with grass, leaves, cloth and feathers, up to 18 metres above the ground. 4-5 eggs.

Egg: Actual Size

Cedar Waxwing
Bombycilla cedrorum

Observation Calendar
J F M A M J J A S O N D

Male/Female: Crested brown head with black mask running from black bill, through eyes, to behind head; white outline around mask; back brown; chest and belly yellow-brown; wings black-grey with white edges; wings and tail have red tips; rump white.

Did you know? The name derives from the fact that their wings and tail look as though they have been dipped in red wax.

Voice: Extremely high-pitched *seeee*.
Food: A variety of berries.
Nest/Eggs: Loose woven cup of grass, twigs, cotton fibre and string, lined with small roots, fine grass and down, in open wooded areas in tree or shrub, 2-6 metres above ground. 4-5 eggs.

Blue-winged Warbler

Vermivora pinus

Observation Calendar

J F M A M J J A S O N D

Male: Bright yellow head, chin, chest and belly; black line through eyes; blue-black wings and tail with white banding along wings; grey back; feet and legs black; black bill.
Female: Similar markings to male but paler overall.

Voice: Low-pitched *buzzzzz* in 2 notes descending, sounds like "blue-winged."
Food: Variety of insects and spiders.
Nest/Eggs: Cup-like, built of leaves, grasses, and vines in a tangle near ground. 4-7 eggs.

Nashville Warbler

Vermivora ruficapilla

Size Identification

Beak

Observation Calendar

J F M A M J J A S O N D

Male/Female: Thin, very pointed bill; head and neck bluish grey; eye-ring white; upper parts olive green; underparts yellow, white on belly.

Voice: Calls include *see it see it see it*, and *ti ti ti ti ti*.
Food: A variety of insects.
Nest/Eggs: Nest of moss or bark lined with grass and hair, on ground. 4-5 eggs.

Nesting Location

Yellow Warbler

Dendroica petechia

Observation Calendar

J F M A M J J A S O N D

Male: Yellow throat and chest; olive back; wings and tail dark olive with yellow highlights; chest barred with chestnut stripes; bill and feet reddish black.
Female: Similar to male only darker and lacks chestnut markings below.

Voice: A sweet and rapid *tsee, tsee, tsee, tsee, titi-wee.*
Food: Insects with large quantities of caterpillars, beetles and moths. Young birds are fed earthworms as well.
Nest/Eggs: Cup of milkweed, hair, down and fine grasses, built in upright fork of tree or bush. 3-6 eggs.

Chestnut-sided Warbler

Dendroica pensylvanica

Male: Bright lemon-yellow crown with chestnut down sides of breast; black band running through eyes from black bill; black and white banding on back with yellow tinting; wings and tail black with white edges; feet and legs black; chin and belly white.

Female: Similar to male except mask is duller and chestnut on sides is reduced.

Did you know? Audubon found these birds to be rare, but with the clearing of woodland, sightings have increased.

Voice: A territorial song — *sweet sweet sweet I so sweet*.

Food: A variety of insects including caterpillars, moths and beetles.

Nest/Eggs: Loose cup of stems, grass and plant down, lined with grass and hair, in briar tangles, hedges or shrubs, up to 2 metres above ground. 3-5 eggs.

Magnolia Warbler

Dendroica magnolia

Observation Calendar
J F M A M J J A S O N D

Male: Grey head with small eyebrow stripe of white above eyes; black mask; yellow chin; chest and belly yellow with black banding; back grey with black; wings and tail grey with white edges; two white wing bars; white rump.
Female: Similar to male except banding on chest is narrower; face is grey without black mask and white eyebrow; white eye-ring.

Voice: A short melodic song — *weeta weeta weeta wee.*
Food: A variety of insects and spiders.
Nest/Eggs: Nest is a loosely built cup of grass, moss and weed stalks, lined with dark roots, in small conifers along the edge of wooded areas and in gardens. 3-5 eggs.

Black-throated Blue Warbler

Dendroica caerulescens

Size Identification

Beak

Observation Calendar

J F M A M J J A S O N D

Male: Blue-grey head and back; black face mask with black bill; chest white; wings and tail black with white edges; feet and legs black.

Female: Olive-brown head, back and wings with lighter tone on chin, chest and belly; black bill; thin buff eyebrows; feet and legs black; wings and tail olive-brown with white edges.

Voice: A husky song, "I am soo lazzzzy," and a call that is a flat *tip*.

Food: A variety of insects, fruits and seeds taken mainly on ground or low lying branches.

Nest/Eggs: Bulky cup of spiderweb, dead wood, twigs, leaves and grass, lined with dark rootlets in tree or shrub close to ground. 3-5 eggs.

Nesting Location

Yellow-rumped Warbler

Dendroica coronata

Size Identification

Beak

Observation Calendar

J F M A M J J A S O N D

Male/Female: *Spring:* Yellow rump and yellow patch on either side of chest; yellow crown set against grey head; black mask running from black bill; back grey with black banding; wings and tail black with white edges; two white wing bars; chin white; chest white with black band; feet and legs charcoal; white eyebrows. *Fall:* Similar but duller markers, no black mask, more brown and buff overall.

Voice: Song is light musical notes. Call is *cheeeck*.
Food: A variety of insects and fruit.
Nest/Eggs: Deep cup of twigs, bark, plant down and fibres, lined with hair feather and fine grass, in tree or shrub near trunk. 3-5 eggs.

Nesting Location

Egg: Actual Size

Black-throated Green Warbler

Dendroica virens

Size Identification

Beak

Observation Calendar
J F M A M J J A S O N D

Male: Olive head and back; yellow around eyes and on cheeks; black throat and chest changing to speckled black on white on belly and chest; black banding along sides of belly; wings and tail are black with white edging; two white bars on wings; feet and legs brown-black; white vent at base of tail.
Female: Yellow on throat with minimal black.

Voice: Song has a variety of accents — *zee zee zee zuu zee*, and sounds like "sleep sleep little one sleep."
Food: Variety of insects and fruit.
Nest/Eggs: Compact cup of fine bark, twigs, grass, lichens and spiderweb, lined with hair, fur, feathers and small roots, in tree or shrub, 1-25 metres above ground. 3-5 eggs.

Nesting Location

Pine Warbler

Dendroica pinus

Observation Calendar
J F M A M J J A S O N D

Male: Bright yellow chin, chest and belly; dark wings with white banding; short black pointed beak; light streaking along sides; green head and back; tail black with yellow highlights; feet and legs dark; yellow ring around eyes.
Female: Dull greyish brown head and back; yellowish chin, chest and belly.

Voice: Melodic trill. Call is *chiiip*.
Food: Insects, spiders, fruit, berries and pine seeds.
Nest/Eggs: Pine needles shaped into cup along with pieces of bark and weeds. Always in a pine tree. 3-5 eggs.

109

Black-and-white Warbler

Mniotilta varia

Size Identification

Beak

Observation Calendar

J F M A M J J A S O N D

Male: Black-and-white striped from crown down entire body length; feet and legs charcoal; bill is thin and black with thin yellow line at mouth opening.
Female: Similar to the male except striping on chest and belly is grey and white, throat is white.

Did you know? The Black-and-white Warbler is one of the earliest migrants to return in spring.

Nesting Location

Voice: Seven or more squeaky calls — *weesee, weesee, weesee, weesee, weesee, weesee, weesee.*
Food: A variety of insects, mainly gypsy moths and tent caterpillars.
Nest/Eggs: Cup built of leaves, grass, hair and bark, at base of tree or near a boulder. 4-5 eggs.

American Redstart

Setophaga ruticilla

Size Identification

Beak

Observation Calendar

J F M A M J J A S O N D

Male: Black overall with large orange bands on wings and outer tail feathers; bright red/orange patch on side of chest; belly white; feet and legs black.

Female: Overall olive-grey with large yellow bands on wings and tail; white eye-ring, broken; yellow on sides of white chest; white belly; feet and legs black.

Voice: Song is a series of high-pitched thin notes ending downward. Call is *chip.*

Food: A variety of insects, wild berries and seeds.

Nest/Eggs: Compact woven cup built with plant down and grass, lined with weeds, hair and feathers, covered on the outside with lichens, plant down and spiderweb, in woodlands and swamps. 4 eggs.

Nesting Location

Egg: Actual Size

Ovenbird
Seiurus aurocapillus

Size Identification

Beak

Observation Calendar
J F M A M J J A S O N D

Male/Female: Olive overall with distinctive mark on head that is orange outlined in black, running from bill to the back of the neck; chest white with black speckles; bill dark on top with yellow on underside; black eyes surrounded by white.

Voice: A progressively louder *teecher, teecher, teecher, teecher.*
Food: Snails, slugs, worms, spiders and most other insects.
Nest/Eggs: Covered bowl, with side entry made of dead leaves, grass, moss and bark, lined with small roots, fibres and hair, on ground in depression. 3-5 eggs.

Nesting Location

Egg: Actual Size   112

Common Yellowthroat

Geothlypis trichas

Observation Calendar

J F M A M J J A S O N D

Male: Yellow chin, chest and belly contrast with a dark black mask, which runs from bill, around eyes, to lower neck; white line blends into an olive head, back, wings and tail; feet and legs grey.

Female: Light brown without the distinctive mask.

Voice: A very high-pitched song — *witchity, witchity, witchity* — that is heavily accented.

Food: Caterpillars, beetles, ants and other small insects.

Nest/Eggs: Bulky cup of grass, reeds, leaves and moss, lined with grass and hair, on or near ground, in weed stalks or low bushes. 3-5 eggs.

Scarlet Tanager
Piranga olivacea

Size Identification

Beak

Observation Calendar
J F M A M J J A S O N D

Male: Scarlet red from head to rump with dark black wings and tail; bill is pale grey; feet and legs dark.
Female: Olive-yellow overall with black-grey wings and tail.

Voice: Call is a *chip burr*, while its song is a buzzing *querit, queer, queery, querit, queer* that is well spaced out.
Food: A variety of insects and fruit.
Nest/Eggs: Stout cup nest on farthest branches in tree or shrub, sometimes far from the ground. 3-5 eggs.

Nesting Location

Eastern Towhee

Pipilo erythrophthalmus

Observation Calendar

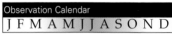

J F M A M J J A S O N D

Male: Distinctive black head with black bill; rust-red sides and vent; white belly; feet and legs pinkish-grey; black back with white banding; long black tail with white oval-shaped underparts.

Female: Similar to male but with brown head, back and tail; white belly.

Voice: Whistle followed by a trill in 2 notes. Sounds like *"drink your tea."* Call is a quick *chewink.*

Food: Variety of insects, snakes, lizards, weeds and spiders.

Nest/Eggs: Built of twigs and leaves with softer grasses lining inside placed in depression in ground. 2-6 eggs.

115

American Tree Sparrow

Spizella arborea

Size Identification

Beak

Backyard Feeder

J F M A M J J A S O N D

Male/Female: Rust on top of head with light grey face, rust band running through eyes; chin, chest and belly grey with a faint dark grey spot on chest; wings and tail brown and black with white edge; two white wing bars; short pointed bill is grey on top with yellow underside; feet and legs are red-black; rump grey.

Voice: Call is *te el wit.*
Food: A variety of weed seeds and tree seeds.
Nest/Eggs: Cup nest, low in tree and shrub. 4 eggs.

Nesting Location

Egg: Actual Size

Chipping Sparrow

Spizella passerina

Size Identification

Beak

Backyard Feeder

Nesting Location

Observation Calendar

J F M A M J J A S O N D

Male/Female: *Summer:* Bright rust crown with grey face that has a black band running through each eye; short pointed bill is black; chin white changing to grey for chest and belly; feet and legs pink; white eyebrows; wings and tail dark with brown and white edges; brown banding with black on back. *Winter:* Rust crown becomes duller, turning brown with black streaks; bill is pale yellow and black; eyebrows change to buff; underside changes to buff.

Voice: Song is short trill.
Food: A variety of insects on the ground and occasionally snatches flying insects.
Nest/Eggs: Cup built with grass, weed stalks and small roots, lined with hair and grass, low in tree or shrub, up to 8 metres above ground. 4 eggs.

Field Sparrow
Spizella pusilla

Size Identification

Beak

Backyard Feeder

Observation Calendar

J F M A M J J A S O N D

Male/Female: Overall brown with grey speckles; reddish-brown cap; distinctive white eye-ring; bright pink bill; feet and legs pinkish-grey; tail dark with brown highlights; white vent and lower belly.

Nesting Location

Voice: Whistles descending and gradually increasing in speed. Calls are *chip* and trills.
Food: Various insects and seeds. May visit feeders if seeds have fallen to ground.
Nest/Eggs: Cup-like, built from a variety of grasses and positioned on ground. 3-4 eggs.

Vesper Sparrow

Pooecetes gramineus

Size Identification

Beak

Backyard Feeder

Observation Calendar

J F M A M J J A S O N D

Male/Female: Light grey overall with very fine streaks of black running down entire body; short pointed bill; feet and legs grey; back banded with black; wings and tail dark grey with white edges; white eye-ring, and small chestnut patch near shoulder; white tail feathers are revealed in flight.

Did you know? The Vesper Sparrow earned its name from its song that may be heard in the evening — at vespers, when evening prayers were said in the monasteries.

Voice: A whistle of two beats, with the second being higher, followed by trills.
Food: A variety of insects, weed seeds and grains.
Nest/Eggs: Depression in ground filled with grass, stalks and small roots, and lined with the same. 4 eggs.

Nesting Location

119

Egg: Actual Size

Savannah Sparrow
Passerculus sandwichensis

Male/Female: Black, brown and white stripe on head; back brown with black banding; chin and chest streaked with black and brown; wings and tail black with brown edges; tail is notched; bright yellow eyebrows; feet and legs red; short pointed bill; white eye-ring.

Voice: A faint, lisping *tsit tsit tsit tseeeee tsaaaay.*
Food: Main diet consists of weed seeds, but will eat a variety of insects, spiders and snails.
Nest/Eggs: Scratched hollow in ground filled with grass, lined with finer grass, hair and small roots. 3-6 eggs.

Song Sparrow

Melospiza melodia

Size Identification

Beak

Backyard Feeder

Nesting Location

Egg: Actual Size

Observation Calendar

J F M A M J J A S O N D

Male/Female: Brown head and back streaked with black; whitish eyebrows extending to back of neck; brown band running through eyes; chin, chest and belly are white with brown-black banding running down to lower belly; short pointed bill is brown on top with paler underside; red-brown crown with central white stripe; wings and tail brown with white edges; feet and legs pale brown; long rounded tail.

Did you know? Thoreau interpreted this sparrow's song as "Maids! Maids! Maids! hang up your teakettle-ettle-ettle."

Voice: A variety of calls including *tsip* and *tchump*. Song is a variety of rich notes.
Food: Various insects, weed seeds and fruit.
Nest/Eggs: Cup close to ground made with weeds, leaves and bark, lined with grass roots and hair, in tree or shrub, less than 4 metres from ground. 3-5 eggs.

Swamp Sparrow
Melospiza georgiana

Beak

Observation Calendar
J F M A M J J A S O N D

Male/Female: *Summer:* Top of head is reddish brown and black; black line through each eye; pale grey eyebrows; black bill is small and sharp; chin and chest white-grey with rust along sides; back brown with black banding; wings and tail feathers brown with black ends and white edges; feet and legs pink. *Winter:* Similar to summer but both sides of chest turn darker brown and top of head is streaked with black and brown with grey central stripe.

Put on your hip waders to spot this bird. They spend their summers near swamps and bogs.

Voice: Song is an unbroken musical trill. Call is *chip.*
Food: A variety of insects and seeds.
Nest/Eggs: Bulky cup built with grass, lined with finer grass, in tussock of grass or in low shrub. 3-6 eggs.

Nesting Location

White-throated Sparrow

Zonotrichia albicollis

Size Identification

Beak

Backyard Feeder

Nesting Location

Egg: Actual Size

Observation Calendar

J F M A M J J A S O N D

Male/Female: Top of head is black with white central stripe; white eyebrows on either side with yellow tint at base of bill; black band running through eyes followed by grey cheeks; small white bib under chin; grey chest; grey belly with faint banding; wings and tail feathers black and brown with white edges; back brown-banded with black.

Voice: Whistle is *teeet teeet tetodi tetodi teetodi*. Calls are *tseet*.
Food: A variety of insects, grains, weed seeds and fruit.
Nest/Eggs: Cup built of grass, small roots, pine needles, twigs, bark and moss, lined with small roots, hair and grass. 3-5 eggs.

Dark-eyed Junco
Junco hyemalis

Size Identification

Beak

Backyard Feeder

Observation Calendar
J F M A M J J A S O N D

Male: Dark charcoal overall with white belly; short sharp bill; feet and legs pink; tail has white outer feathers that can be seen in flight.
Female: May be slightly paler than male.

Did you know? Although there are many different sub-species, the slate-coloured is the only one found in the region.

Voice: Song is a trill in short phrases. Calls are *tsip, zeeet* or *keew keew.*
Food: A variety of insects, weed seeds and wild fruit.
Nest/Eggs: Large and compact nest built with grass, rootlets and hair, lined with hair, concealed low to or on the ground. 4-5 eggs.

Nesting Location

Egg: Actual Size

124

Northern Cardinal

Cardinalis cardinalis

Size Identification

Beak

Backyard Feeder

Observation Calendar

J F M A M J J A S O N D

Male: Brilliant red overall with a stout red-orange bill, crested head; black mask beginning at base of bill resembling a small bib; feet dark red.

Female: Buff and grey with hints of bright red on crest, wings and back. Stout red-orange bill with black mask beginning at base of bill (bib may appear smaller), feet are dark red.

Did you know? The cardinal gets its name from its bright red colour, which resembles that of the robes and hat of a Roman Catholic cardinal.

Voice: Song is a series of repeated whistles — *wheit wheit wheit, cheer cheer cheer.* Also *chip.*

Food: Seeds, fruits, grains and various insects.

Nest/Eggs: Woven cup of twigs, vines, leaves and grass, 2-3 metres above ground, in dense shrubbery. 2-5 eggs.

Nesting Location

125

Egg: Actual Size

Rose-breasted Grosbeak

Pheucticus ludovicianus

Observation Calendar

J F M A M J J A S O N D

Male: Large, pale bill with black head; red V shape on chest; belly white with rust on either side close to wing; wings and tail black; white at edges of tail feathers visible in flight; white patches on wings; rump white; feet and legs charcoal.
Female: Buff eyebrows that extend to back of neck; brown head and back with shade of black; wings and tail brown with white edges; two white wing bars; chest and belly streaked brown; feet and legs charcoal.

Did you know? The Rose-breasted Grosbeak is a fierce competitor when mating, clashing violently with other males. However, when it comes time to sitting on the nest, the males have been known to sing.

Voice: Similar to a robin, but rapid notes that are a continuous *cheer-e-ly cheer-e-ly.* Call is *chink chink.*
Food: A variety of insects, tree buds, fruit and wild seeds.
Nest/Eggs: Woven grass cup in fork of deciduous tree or shrub, close to the ground. 3-6 eggs.

126

Indigo Bunting

Passerina cyanea

Beak

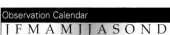

Observation Calendar
J F M A M J J A S O N D

Male: Medium to deep turquoise blue overall; wide, sharp, grey beak; feet and legs black; wings and tail dark with blue highlights.
Female: Soft brown overall; buff sides and belly; faint wing bands; short conical grey beak.

Voice: Rapid series of whistles that are short and paired together — *tse tsee tew tew*. Call is short *spiit*.
Food: Insects, seeds, grain, berries.
Nest/Eggs: Compact woven cup built from stems, grasses and leaves, lined with down in thick vegetation. 2-6 eggs.

Nesting Location

Egg: Actual Size

Size Identification

Beak

Bobolink
Dolichonyx oryzivorus

Nesting Location

Observation Calendar
J F M A M J J A S O N D

Male: *Summer:* Black overall with pale yellow patch on back of head; back black changing to large white patch down to rump; wings have white patches and edges; bill black. In flight: white rump is revealed. Tail has sharp pointed feathers.
Female/Male: *Winter:* brown and buff overall with black streaks over top of head; legs red.

Did you know? These birds need a hayfield habitat to survive. Studies show that most of the young will die when farmers' fields are mown before they have a chance to fledge.

Voice: Song is a light phrase that increases in pitch and has been described as *Bob o link, bob o link spink spank spink.* Usually sings in flight. Call is metallic *clink.*
Food: A variety of insects and weed seeds.
Nest/Eggs: Slight hollow in ground with bulky gathering of grass and weed stalks. Lined with fine grass in areas near water and within waterside plants. 4-7 eggs.

Red-winged Blackbird

Agelaius phoeniceus

Observation Calendar

J F M A M J J A S O N D

Male: Black overall with distinctive red shoulder patch bordered with light yellow at bottom.
Female: Brown with buff eyebrows and chin; chest and belly buff streaked with dark brown; wings and tail feathers brown with buff edges.

Did you know? Red-winged Blackbirds are prolific breeders, sometimes breeding three times in one season. They are seen in freshwater marshes.

Voice: Song is *ocaaleee ocaalee.*
Food: A variety of insects and weed seeds.
Nest/Eggs: Bulky cup built of leaves, rushes, grass, rootlets, moss and milkweed fibre, lined with grass, in tall waterside plants. 3-4 eggs.

129

Eastern Meadowlark
Sturnella magna

Size Identification

Beak

Backyard Feeder

Birdhouse Nester

Nesting Location

Observation Calendar
J F M A M J J A S O N D

Male/Female: Bright yellow chin and throat separated by a V-shaped black collar; black on top of head with grey cheeks; yellow and black band runs through eyes; sides white with black sidebars; back and wings black and brown with white edges; feet and legs grey; pale bill is long and thin with grey underside.

Voice: Song is *teee yuuu teee yaar* repeated 2-8 times.
Food: A variety of insects including grubs, beetles, grasshoppers and caterpillars. Also eats seeds and grains.
Nest/Eggs: Bulky cup in hollow on the ground in pastures, fields and marshes. Dome-shaped with a roof of interwoven grasses. 3-5 eggs.

Common Grackle

Quiscalus quiscula

Size Identification

Beak

Backyard Feeder

Observation Calendar

J F M A M J J A S O N D

Male: Overall iridescent black and purple; bright yellow eyes; black bill long and sharp; feet and legs are charcoal grey; long tail.

Female: Similar but duller iridescent colouring, tail is shorter.

Did you know? Flocks in the thousands gather on fields and cause a lot of damage to farmers' crops.

Voice: Chatter is a metallic and rasping *grideleeeeek*. Calls are *chak chah*.

Food: A variety of ground insects, seeds, grains, minnows, rodents and crayfish.

Nest/Eggs: Loose bulky cup built with weed stalks, twigs, grass, debris, lined with feather and grass, in conifer trees or shrubs. Will occasionally use an osprey's nest. Prefers to nest in colonies. 3-6 eggs.

Nesting Location

131

Egg: Actual Size

Brown-headed Cowbird

Molothrus ater

Size Identification

Beak

Observation Calendar

J F M A M J J A S O N D

Male: Brown head, glossy black overall; feet and legs black; sharp black bill.

Female: Overall grey with dark brown wings and tail; faint buff streaking on chest down to lower belly, feet and legs are black.

Did you know? Molothrus ater, the Cowbird's scientific name, means dark, greedy beggar, an apt name for a bird that leaves its eggs for other birds to hatch.

Voice: A squeaky *weee titi*.

Food: A variety of insects, weed seeds, grains and grass.

Nest/Eggs: Lays eggs in nests of other birds. 1 egg.

Nesting Location

Egg: Actual Size

Orchard Oriole

Icterus spurius

Beak

Backyard Feeder

Observation Calendar

J F M A M J J A S O N D

Male: Black head and back; long, sharp black beak; chestnut belly and rump; long black tail; feet and legs black; black wings with one wing bar.
Female: Olive-green overall; yellow belly and chest; wings black with two wing bars.

Voice: Quick progression of whistled notes. Call is a quick *chuck*.
Food: Insects, fruit, sugar solutions and tree blossoms.
Nest/Eggs: Suspended pouch woven with grass and lined with fine material. 3-7 eggs.

Nesting Location

Egg: Actual Size

Baltimore Oriole

Icterus galbula

Size Identification

Beak

Backyard Feeder

Observation Calendar
J F M A M J J A S O N D

Male: Black head; bright orange body; black wings with orange spur and white banding; tail is black with orange along edges; legs and feet grey; long sharp grey beak.
Female: Browner than male with olive-yellow on rump; orange-yellow chest and belly; head and back mix of black, orange and brown; throat blotched; tail brown-orange.

Did you know? Baltimore Orioles can be attracted to feeders with orange slices or sugar solutions.

Nesting Location

Voice: Song is a note whistled 4-8 times. Call is a two-note *teetoo* and rapid chatter *ch ch ch ch*.
Food: Insects, flower nectar, fruit.
Nest/Eggs: Plant fibre that hangs from branches. 4-6 eggs.

House Finch

Carpodacus mexicanus

Beak

Backyard Feeder

Observation Calendar

J F M A M J J A S O N D

Male: Red crown, chin and chest, which changes to buff at belly; wings and tail brown; feet and legs grey; grey bill; white undertail; dark brown banding around the sides.
Female: All greyish brown with faint banding down the sides.

Voice: Musical warble ending with *jeeeeer*.
Food: Weed seeds, fruit, buds.
Nest/Eggs: Cup of lined weed and grass, roots, feathers, string and twigs, 1-2 metres above ground. 4-5 eggs.

Nesting Location

Egg: Actual Size

American Goldfinch

Carduelis tristis

Size Identification

Beak

Backyard Feeder

Observation Calendar

J F M A M J J A S O N D

Male: *Summer:* Bright yellow overall with black forehead and yellow bill; black wings with white bands; tail black with white edges; rump white; feet and legs red. *Winter:* Similar, but bright yellow is replaced by grey with hints of yellow.

Female/Male: *Winter:* Similar except overall olive brown with yellow highlights.

Voice: Sing as they fly with a succession of chips and twitters, *per chic o ree per chic o ree.*

Food: A variety of insects, but mostly interested in thistle and weed seeds.

Nest/Eggs: Neat cup built with fibres woven together, lined with thistle and feather down, in leafy tree or shrubs in upright branches, 1-5 metres above ground. 4-6 eggs.

Nesting Location

House Sparrow

Passer domesticus

Size Identification

Beak

Backyard Feeder

Birdhouse Nester

Nesting Location

Observation Calendar
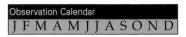

J F M A M J J A S O N D

Male: Grey crown with rich brown from eye to back; white cheeks; wings and tail striped with black; two distinct white wing bands; rump grey; throat and chest black, which turns grey at belly; bill black; feet and legs pink.
Female: Dull brown with buff chin, chest and belly; light buff-coloured eyebrows and yellow/grey bill.

Did you know? In 1850, 8 pairs of House Sparrows were brought to North America from Europe to help control cankerworms in crops. The first attempt failed, but this sparrow has now become one of the most common birds in cities and towns.

Voice: Repeated *chureep, chirup*.
Food: Insects, seeds, grains and food waste.
Nest/Eggs: Takes over nests from other birds. Usually a large untidy ball of grass, weeds, some hair, feathers. 3-7 eggs.

Egg: Actual Size

Checklist of Birds

This checklist follows the same sequence as the book. Use these pages to record the date and place of bird sightings.

☐ Common Loon *18*
Date: _____
Place: _____

☐ Double-crested Cormorant *19*
Date: _____
Place: _____

☐ Great Blue Heron *20*
Date: _____
Place: _____

☐ Turkey Vulture *21*
Date: _____
Place: _____

☐ Canada Goose *22*
Date: _____
Place: _____

☐ Mute Swan *23*
Date: _____
Place: _____

☐ Tundra Swan *24*
Date: _____
Place: _____

☐ Wood Duck *25*
Date: _____
Place: _____

☐ Gadwall *26*
Date: _____
Place: _____

☐ American Wigeon *27*
Date: _____
Place: _____

☐ American Black Duck *28*
Date: _____
Place: _____

☐ Mallard *29*
Date: _____
Place: _____

☐ Blue-winged Teal *30*
Date: _____
Place: _____

☐ Northern Pintail *31*
Date: _____
Place: _____

☐ Green-winged Teal *32*
Date: _____
Place: _____

☐ Ring-necked Duck *33*
Date: _____
Place: _____

☐ Bufflehead *34*
Date: _____
Place: _____

☐ Hooded Merganser *35*
Date: _____
Place: _____

☐ Common Merganser *36*
Date: _____
Place: _____

☐ Ruddy Duck *37*
Date: _____
Place: _____

☐ Osprey *38*
Date: _____
Place: _____

☐ Bald Eagle *39*
Date: _____
Place: _____

☐ Sharp-shinned Hawk 40
Date: _____
Place: _____

☐ Red-tailed Hawk 41
Date: _____
Place: _____

☐ Rough-legged Hawk 42
Date: _____
Place: _____

☐ American Kestrel 43
Date: _____
Place: _____

☐ Peregrine Falcon 44
Date: _____
Place: _____

☐ Ring-necked Pheasant 45
Date: _____
Place: _____

☐ Ruffed Grouse 46
Date: _____
Place: _____

☐ Wild Turkey 47
Date: _____
Place: _____

☐ Virginia Rail 48
Date: _____
Place: _____

☐ Sora 49
Date: _____
Place: _____

☐ American Coot 50
Date: _____
Place: _____

☐ Killdeer 51
Date: _____
Place: _____

☐ Spotted Sandpiper 52
Date: _____
Place: _____

☐ Ring-billed Gull 53
Date: _____
Place: _____

☐ Herring Gull 54
Date: _____
Place: _____

☐ Great Black-backed Gull 55
Date: _____
Place: _____

☐ Rock Dove 56
Date: _____
Place: _____

☐ Mourning Dove 57
Date: _____
Place: _____

☐ Black-billed Cuckoo 58
Date: _____
Place: _____

☐ Yellow-billed Cuckoo 59
Date: _____
Place: _____

☐ Eastern Screech-Owl 60
Date: _____
Place: _____

☐ Great Horned Owl 61
Date: _____
Place: _____

☐ Chimney Swift 62
Date: _____
Place: _____

☐ Ruby-throated Hummingbird 63
Date: _____
Place: _____

☐ Belted Kingfisher 64
Date: _____
Place: _____

☐ Red-headed Woodpecker *65*
Date: _____
Place: _____

☐ Red-bellied Woodpecker *66*
Date: _____
Place: _____

☐ Downy Woodpecker *67*
Date: _____
Place: _____

☐ Hairy Woodpecker *68*
Date: _____
Place: _____

☐ Northern Flicker *69*
Date: _____
Place: _____

☐ Eastern Wood-Pewee *70*
Date: _____
Place: _____

☐ Least Flycatcher *71*
Date: _____
Place: _____

☐ Eastern Phoebe *72*
Date: _____
Place: _____

☐ Great Crested Flycatcher *73*
Date: _____
Place: _____

☐ Eastern Kingbird *74*
Date: _____
Place: _____

☐ Warbling Vireo *75*
Date: _____
Place: _____

☐ Red-eyed Vireo *76*
Date: _____
Place: _____

☐ Blue Jay *77*
Date: _____
Place: _____

☐ American Crow *78*
Date: _____
Place: _____

☐ Horned Lark *79*
Date: _____
Place: _____

☐ Purple Martin *80*
Date: _____
Place: _____

☐ Tree Swallow *81*
Date: _____
Place: _____

☐ Northern Rough-winged Swallow *82*
Date: _____
Place: _____

☐ Bank Swallow *83*
Date: _____
Place: _____

☐ Cliff Swallow *84*
Date: _____
Place: _____

☐ Barn Swallow *85*
Date: _____
Place: _____

☐ Black-capped Chickadee *86*
Date: _____
Place: _____

☐ Red-breasted Nuthatch *87*
Date: _____
Place: _____

☐ White-breasted Nuthatch *88*
Date: _____
Place: _____

☐ Brown Creeper *89*
Date: _____
Place: _____

☐ House Wren *90*
Date: _____
Place: _____

☐ Golden-crowned Kinglet *91*
Date: _____
Place: _____

☐ Ruby-crowned Kinglet *92*
Date: _____
Place: _____

☐ Eastern Bluebird *93*
Date: _____
Place: _____

☐ Veery *94*
Date: _____
Place: _____

☐ Wood Thrush *95*
Date: _____
Place: _____

☐ American Robin *96*
Date: _____
Place: _____

☐ Gray Catbird *97*
Date: _____
Place: _____

☐ Brown Thrasher *98*
Date: _____
Place: _____

☐ European Starling *99*
Date: _____
Place: _____

☐ Cedar Waxwing *100*
Date: _____
Place: _____

☐ Blue-winged Warbler *101*
Date: _____
Place: _____

☐ Nashville Warbler *102*
Date: _____
Place: _____

☐ Yellow Warbler *103*
Date: _____
Place: _____

☐ Chestnut-sided Warbler *104*
Date: _____
Place: _____

☐ Magnolia Warbler *105*
Date: _____
Place: _____

☐ Black-throated Blue
Warbler *106*
Date: _____
Place: _____

☐ Yellow-rumped Warbler *107*
Date: _____
Place: _____

☐ Black-throated Green
Warbler *108*
Date: _____
Place: _____

☐ Pine Warbler *109*
Date: _____
Place: _____

☐ Black-and-white
Warbler *110*
Date: _____
Place: _____

☐ American Redstart *111*
Date: _____
Place: _____

☐ Ovenbird *112*
Date: _____
Place: _____

☐ Common Yellowthroat *113*
Date: _____
Place: _____

☐ Scarlet Tanager *114*
Date: _____
Place: _____

☐ Eastern Towhee *115*
Date: _____
Place: _____

☐ American Tree
Sparrow *116*
Date: _____
Place: _____

☐ Chipping Sparrow *117*
Date: _____
Place: _____

☐ Field Sparrow *118*
Date: _____
Place: _____

☐ Vesper Sparrow *119*
Date: _____
Place: _____

☐ Savannah Sparrow *120*
Date: _____
Place: _____

☐ Song Sparrow *121*
Date: _____
Place: _____

☐ Swamp Sparrow *122*
Date: _____
Place: _____

☐ White-throated
Sparrow *123*
Date: _____
Place: _____

☐ Dark-eyed Junco *124*
Date: _____
Place: _____

☐ Northern Cardinal *125*
Date: _____
Place: _____

☐ Rose-breasted
Grosbeak *126*
Date: _____
Place: _____

☐ Indigo Bunting *127*
Date: _____
Place: _____

☐ Bobolink *128*
Date: _____
Place: _____

☐ Red-winged Blackbird *129*
Date: _____
Place: _____

☐ Eastern Meadowlark *130*
Date: _____
Place: _____

☐ Common Grackle *131*
Date: _____
Place: _____

☐ Brown-headed Cowbird
132
Date: _____
Place: _____

☐ Orchard Oriole *133*
Date: _____
Place: _____

☐ Baltimore Oriole *134*
Date: _____
Place: _____

☐ House Finch *135*
Date: _____
Place: _____

☐ American Goldfinch *136*
Date: _____
Place: _____

☐ House Sparrow *137*
Date: _____
Place: _____

Index